The disconnect between what we believe and how we act—this changes everything. *The Struggle Is Real* is a practical guidebook to help us take God at His word and live lives of freedom and power.

JENNIE ALLEN
Author of *Nothing to Prove*; founder and visionary of the IF:Gathering

Max De Pree used to say that the first task of a leader is to define reality. That is what Nicole Unice has done in *The Struggle Is Real*. But she doesn't just define it, she gives us the hope to cope.

JOHN ORTBERG
Senior pastor of Menlo Church, Menlo Park, California; author of *I'd Like You More If You Were More like Me*

I've known Nicole Unice for nearly a decade, and I can honestly say that if she's anything, Nicole is *real* and she has a *real* passion for others to embrace how *real* God can be in their *real* lives. In *The Struggle Is Real*, Nicole pours out this passion in an accessible read. Turning these pages is like sitting with a safe friend in a sunny spot and coming away with a refreshed perspective on the *real* difference God can make in our lives.

ELISA MORGAN
Speaker; author of *The Beauty of Broken* and *The Prayer Coin*; cohost of *Discover the Word*; president emerita of MOPS International

You're going to love Nicole Unice. She's bright, funny, observant, honest, and fearless about speaking the truth in love. Her advice in *The Struggle Is Real* is practical and doable, full of common sense and uncommon wisdom, and her true-to-life stories give each lesson a solid landing place in our hearts. This isn't a book you simply read; it's a book you *do*, with remarkable results.

LIZ CURTIS HIGGS
Bestselling author of *Bad Girls of the Bible*

Many of us have grown weary of books that offer simplistic steps promising easy transformation. This is not that kind of book. Nicole Unice writes from a deep place of reflection and personal experience about how real is the struggle . . . and how real is the process of true growth and change. I urge you to join her on the journey.

NANCY BEACH
Leadership coach with Slingshot Group; author of *Gifted to Lead: The Art of Leading as a Woman in the Church*

We live in a day when we Instagram our lives to be perceived as more than mundane. We Pinterest our meals and homes to present a perception of the fabulous life. I'm grateful for Nicole's book *The Struggle Is Real* because of the way she uses honesty, humor, and the Word of God to liberate us from the pretense of presenting the perfect life.

DAVID M. BAILEY
Founder and executive director of Arrabon; coauthor of the Race, Class, and the Kingdom of God study series

The Struggle Is Real

The Struggle is Real.

Getting better at life, stronger in faith, and free from the stuff keeping you stuck

Nicole Unice

TYNDALE
MOMENTUM®

The nonfiction imprint of
Tyndale House Publishers, Inc.

Visit Tyndale online at www.tyndale.com.

Visit Tyndale Momentum online at www.tyndalemomentum.com.

Visit the author at nicoleunice.com.

TYNDALE, Tyndale Momentum, and Tyndale's quill logo are registered trademarks of Tyndale House Publishers, Inc. The Tyndale Momentum logo is a trademark of Tyndale House Publishers, Inc. Tyndale Momentum is the nonfiction imprint of Tyndale House Publishers, Inc., Carol Stream, Illinois.

The Struggle Is Real: Getting Better at Life, Stronger in Faith, and Free from the Stuff Keeping You Stuck

Designed by Jennifer Phelps

The author is represented by Chip MacGregor of MacGregor Literary, Inc.

All Scripture quotations, unless otherwise indicated, are taken from the Holy Bible, *New International Version,*® *NIV.*® Copyright © 1973, 1978, 1984, 2011 by Biblica, Inc.® (Some quotations may be from the earlier NIV edition, copyright © 1984.) Used by permission. All rights reserved worldwide. Scripture quotations marked AMP are taken from the Amplified® Bible, copyright © 2015 by The Lockman Foundation. Used by permission. www.Lockman.org. Scripture quotations marked CEV are taken from the Contemporary English Version, copyright © 1991, 1992, 1995 by American Bible Society. Used by permission. Scripture quotations marked ESV are taken from *The Holy Bible,* English Standard Version® (ESV®), copyright © 2001 by Crossway, a publishing ministry of Good News Publishers. Used by permission. All rights reserved. Scripture quotations marked MSG are taken from *THE MESSAGE,* copyright © 1993, 1994, 1995, 1996, 2000, 2001, 2002 by Eugene H. Peterson. Used by permission of NavPress. All rights reserved. Represented by Tyndale House Publishers, Inc. Scripture quotations marked NLT are taken from the *Holy Bible,* New Living Translation, copyright © 1996, 2004, 2015 by Tyndale House Foundation. Used by permission of Tyndale House Publishers, Inc., Carol Stream, Illinois 60188. All rights reserved.

The names and identifying details of some of the individuals whose stories appear in this book have been changed to protect their privacy.

For information about special discounts for bulk purchases, please contact Tyndale House Publishers at csresponse@tyndale.com, or call 1-800-323-9400.

ISBN 978-1-4964-2746-5 (hc)
ISBN 978-1-4964-2747-2 (sc)

Printed in the United States of America

24   23   22   21   20   19   18
7   6   5   4   3   2   1

To all the people who've shared their stories with me over the last twenty years—I am so grateful.
Your words have shaped my life.
You've helped me find a passion for the redeemed story that is available to us all.

Contents

Foreword

There are days when we feel we are close to overcoming those daily struggles and habits that hold us back. There are other days when we feel we'll never get out of our stuck place. And much of the time, no one knows what we are going through.

Nicole Unice understands that most of our struggles will never make the daily news. Nobody knows about our feelings of low self-esteem or our sense of being surrounded by friends but feeling lonely in marriage. Very few people dig deep enough to understand how our childhood experiences have shaped us as adults. Nicole will help you do this and more. *The Struggle Is Real* feels like a crack in the door filled with light. Maybe there is hope for us. Maybe there is a way out.

I have known Nicole for over twenty years. She draws from a deep well of experience and compassion for people. She is a gifted writer and Bible teacher, but most of all, she is a woman of deep faith who loves the Word of God and tells stories that help people feel understood.

In 2 Corinthians 4:17, the apostle Paul writes that "our light and momentary troubles are achieving for us an eternal glory that far outweighs them all." Nicole Unice gets this. She understands that there is purpose and meaning in our struggles. Through her writing, Nicole not only touches the deepest part of us, she offers us tools to get us out of the stuck place and find life again. As a fellow struggler and a pastor for over thirty years, I found myself both laughing and brought to tears as I read, but most of all, this book has given me hope. I think you will find hope too.

Peace,

Pete Bowell
Hope Church
Richmond, Virginia

The "Fine" Line

Before we begin, I need to ask you a question:

How are you?

If you're like me, when asked this at the grocery store or by a friend you haven't seen in a while, your response is usually: "Fine!" After all, we can tick off our big blessings—a roof over our heads, shoes on our feet, dinner on the table. "Fine" almost feels like a required answer, especially for the Christian. After all, since God has done so much for us, shouldn't our leading perspective be gratitude and *shouldn't we be fine?*

Well, yes, but also no.

Fine is a terrible little word. It's neither good nor bad. It doesn't convey excitement or despair. You might as well sigh it out, "I'm fiiiinnnne." *Fine* is a tired, shouldn't-this-be-different kind of word. *Fine* is a good word to use when you are kind of frustrated, kind of bored, kind of okay, kind of stuck. *Fine* is what you say when you wonder if things are supposed to feel as hard as they do even in your so-called "good life."

It's funny how it's the little struggles that often reveal the most about what's really underneath the surface of all this "fine" we claim to be. The other day I was avoiding folding my laundry by finding important things to do, and by "important," I mean scrolling through my Instagram feed like it held the secret to life. Between the puppy pics and the coffee/Bible/#blessed Christian "reality," I came across this:

> I dropped a sock from my laundry, and then leaned over to pick up the sock and somehow dropped all my laundry on the floor, and if that's not a picture of my life, I don't know what is. #thestruggleisreal

Clever lines like these have become cultural signs of our era, giving a glimpse behind the shiny veneer of people's everyday lives. Many are followed by the tagline #thestruggleisreal. Search this hashtag and you'll find the struggle runs over three million posts deep, from complaints about the traffic to grievances at the workplace, from annoying habits to annoying people, from struggles with midterms to mishaps with pets. Here are a few others I found while avoiding household chores:

- My tolerance for idiots is extremely low today. I used to have some immunity built up, but obviously there's a new strain out there.
- I spend a lot of time holding the refrigerator door open looking for answers.

- No, I don't really rise and shine. Most days, I just caffeinate and hope for the best.
- I want buns of steel, but I also want buns of cinnamon.

These are the funny ones—because they are clever and true. But I think if we were to reveal the deeper stuff we struggle with, items with that hashtag might overwhelm the Internet.

Recently, I was rushing to pick up my youngest at school. Multitasking as usual, I was having a heart-to-heart conversation with a friend about a recent conflict he faced while also shoehorning my car into the traffic jam that is the elementary school car-pool line. As I waited my turn, I continued to wax on to my younger leader friend about the importance of assuming the best in people, turning the other cheek, and seeking forgiveness. I was on a roll.

All of a sudden, the woman running the car-pool line gestured violently at me, ordering me to roll down my window. (Disclaimer: It felt like a violent gesture to me. *At the time.*) I ended the call, dropped my phone in my lap and smiled out the window as I chirped, "I'm here to pick up my little guy!" I used my best doting, loving, baby-book scrapbooking mom voice.

She looked down at me, closing her fist around her very professional lanyard name tag. "You don't have a pass, *ma'am.* You can't be in the car-pool line. You need to park and walk in."

Okay—she was looking down at me because I was in a sedan and she was standing, but in my heart I knew what was really going on. I knew she was also *looking down* at me, judging me for my phone calls and distraction and disrespect of car-pool protocol like I was a bad mom, *the one who should never have had kids if I was going to act like mothering was a side hustle to real life.*

Given the intense level of conflict I felt between this lady and me in the 1.8 seconds we interacted, you can understand why I glared back at her, told her that I had sent in a note that morning, and rolled my eyes. *And how dare you "ma'am" me, ma'am!* I thought as I drove away. Once I'd parked the car, I slammed the door and stomped inside to grab my kid. I'm not proud to admit that, once back in the car, I drove slowly by the car-pool line so my son could identify the staff member by name and position. I had devised an elaborate plan to expose her as a condescending and judgmental shrew to the entire elementary school community.

Just for the record:

Yes, this really happened.

No, I am not proud of this moment.

Yes, I realize the irony of counseling my friend on the wisdom of grace and forgiveness while simultaneously deconstructing the entire moral fabric of the poor elementary schoolteacher trying to do her job.

Yes, I realize how spiritually bankrupt I was to involve my son, who may or may not have tried to find her name on the school's website when we came home.

Yes, that was the point when I realized what an abject failure I had been as mother that day.

And if you are still wondering, do I think I'm "fine"? Well, no. I am not fine.

When we use the phrase "the struggle is real," we are acknowledging the chasm that often exists between what we *think* and how we really *feel*. Our minds tell us that life will inevitably be difficult and confusing, at least sometimes. But when we experience the difficult and confusing, we *feel* as if something must be terribly wrong. It doesn't matter that those difficult and confusing moments feel minor in the grand scheme of life—because those little struggles dig into a deeper place in our souls. Those little struggles lead us to wonder if we really have what it takes to make it in our lives, or if maybe we missed an important class somewhere about how to actually be a joyful and free human being.

Wow, you might be thinking, *all of this is behind what happened to you in the car-pool line?* I think whatever struggle your car-pool line is, it is just a scene in the larger story of your life. The struggle inside of you, the struggle around you, the struggle between you and others—all of it is a symbol of a much deeper longing that won't be satisfied by a "fine" life.

Yep, the struggle is definitely real. The three million posts for #thestruggleisreal certainly hit the gap between real life and the good life, but to make it much more real, here are a few we'll cover together:

- Life is way harder than I thought it would be, but I feel bad saying that because someone always has it worse than I do.
- There are some things about the way I think and act that I don't think could ever change.

- I spend most of the time somewhere between kind of resentful and downright bitter, with occasional moments of grudging acceptance sprinkled in.
- I really don't know if God is interested in my life, and even if He is, I don't know how to hear from Him.
- My family is so dysfunctional—and I fit right in.
- If you think Lord Voldemort is harsh, you should meet my inner critic.
- I don't know when it's time to move on, so I just stay stuck.

We laugh at the humor and the heart of the first set of #thestruggleisreal quotes, and perhaps cringe at the honesty of the second. But this is reality! In the midst of the hard, heavy, and confusing, however, we have a God who has addressed this reality and has provided a way for us to not only understand life, but to grow stronger and smarter through it all.

God's Word is clear that when we choose to follow Him, we should expect to be changed—not a little, but *entirely transformed*. God's kind of change doesn't make our lives perfect—but it does make them expansive. He offers us lives of freedom and space rather than confinement and striving. He who can calm the storm, raise the dead, and mystify the wisdom of the world still chooses to enter into individual lives with such humility that we often don't know it's happened until we look back and realize He's been there for a long time. If your experiences are leading to *anything less* than full transformation in your heart, in your relationships, and in the story of your past and your future, then I can't wait to do this work together.

We begin this journey in that gap between our "just fine" lives and the truly good lives we are seeking. I like to imagine us having this conversation on a great hike together when we come upon a break in the trail—a deep and muddy ditch in the middle of the path. I jump right into the ditch and am calling to you from the bottom. You are standing above, wondering why in the world anyone would jump in. It's muddy and dirty and probably a little smelly, too, and it looks like it's going to take a lot of work to get to the other side.

But I'm calling you down because I know it's the only way back up. Christ is here ahead of us, and He promises to lead us out. You can stand at the edge of the ditch for as long as you'd like. You can try to find a way around. You can try to jump over. You can try to turn back. But at the end of the day, the only way forward is the way down. You see, I've come to such a ravine more than once on my own journey. I've learned that the ditches are important. I've also learned that the struggles those ditches represent are not just real, they are also *good*. I've learned those hindrances and annoyances and circumstances aren't obstacles keeping us *from* freedom, but they are the very substances God uses to form our character and move us *toward* freedom. The struggles in our lives that leave us feeling stuck, restless, or confused become the trenches where we work out the important stuff of life— where we learn how to overcome everyday frustrations, messy relationships, and our lack of joy and purpose—to become people of honesty, depth, and strength.

So here's the truth: If you are looking for a book that helps you escape reality, this probably isn't the one for you.

But if you are looking for practical, real-life help for the stuff that bothers you—the stuff you wish didn't feel so hard but actually does—well then, welcome to the party. Some parts may be tough, but the beauty is that the struggle is real for all of us. Together, we can walk forward shoulder to shoulder, supporting one another when we need it and giving a karate kick in the rear when it's deserved. Along the way, I hope you'll feel understood and celebrated for your whole story—especially in the struggles. I hope we can laugh together about the crazy ways we live and act and view the world. Most of all, I hope we will resolve to believe that the struggle is real and the struggle is *good*.

Nicole

PS: Getting to the roots of our struggles is easier when we let friends walk alongside us. In fact, the Bible commands us to "carry each other's burdens, and in this way you will fulfill the law of Christ" (Galatians 6:2). With that in mind, I hope you'll consider gathering some friends and going through the book together. There's also a companion study and video series that we've put together to guide you. (See page 257 for more details.)

The Struggle between the Stories

I believe that God has written a story line for each one of us that integrates all of the random and frustrating and confusing struggles—both little and big—into a life of wholeness and purpose. I believe in the power of God to change our lives and to untangle the confused plotlines in the deepest parts of us. I know it because I'm watching Him do this in my own life. I know it because God promises to change us in ways that are much deeper than simply acknowledging our need of a Savior while continuing to remain trapped in the same old patterns.

I've met men and women in every phase of faith who are new to the idea of transformation, who are still caught up in their old stories and whose actions and choices reflect their old way of thinking. I've met people who love the *idea* of God's love but haven't actually known Jesus in their lives. Without even being aware of it, all of these people are stuck, faking transformation instead of actually experiencing it. But the real God is far too big, too loving, and too powerful to remain confined by our predetermined boundaries. And it's in the very places where the struggle is real in your life—the striving, the worry, the restlessness, the discouragement— that you can discover the truth of who He is and the story He wants to write in your life.

The challenge, of course, is transitioning from our old stories, which are full of questions, hurt, and shame, into new stories of joy, meaning, and contentment. In part 1, we'll consider what the "good life"—the one God created us to enjoy—looks like. We will also face a difficult truth: that we've all been hit with soul-sucking pain that doesn't resolve itself nearly as fast or as neatly as an hour-long reality TV show. There is good news here, too, however. God has given us more volition than we realize, and He is infinitely more powerful, loving, and wise than we can fathom.

That is why, as we do the difficult soul work of uncovering and carrying our sin-sick stories to God, we can wait expectantly. Even while on the run from the murder-minded King Saul, David wrote, "I sought the LORD, and he answered me; he delivered me from all my fears. Those who look to him are radiant; their faces are never covered with shame. . . . Taste and see that the LORD is good; blessed is the one who takes refuge in him" (Psalm 34:4-5, 8).

May such confidence be yours and mine as we begin the journey between our old and new stories.

1

The Promise
Real Living

You can tell a lot about a person by the
way they handle three things: a rainy day,
lost luggage, and tangled Christmas lights.

MAYA ANGELOU

The sunlight filtered through the window with a gentle grace, and I woke up with a smile. I knew I had a lot to be grateful for that morning—I was visiting a friend while taking a study leave from work, which meant that I was temporarily not in charge of the groceries, the car pools, the lunches, or the dogs. This kind of break was a rare gift, and with the quiet awakening, the beautiful day, the smell of coffee brewing, and the promise of a couple of meetings that I was looking forward to later that morning, I whispered a quick hallelujah of praise. It was a day full of potential, and I had a particular sense that God was up to something important.

But then I actually got out of bed.

By noon, I felt deflated. I had been caught off guard by the discussion in one meeting, and I'd felt unheard and unseen in the other. My writing—the reason I was away from home in the first place—remained untouched. The sunshine didn't seem so bright as I walked back toward my friend's house that afternoon.

I tried to get in touch with how I was feeling. I remembered taking a college yoga class that taught relaxation techniques. The instructor had us lie down on our backs, palms to the ceiling, and take a "mental scan" of our bodies, from head to toe, looking for places of stress. Trying to help myself, I employed the same yoga-lady technique, but with a focus on a "mental scan" of my soul, looking for why the day had started so well and now I could barely put one foot in front of the other. That only led to some incriminating self-talk. I huffed a sigh of frustration as I thought: *I can't believe I even felt stressed in college. Life is so much more confusing and complicated now that I am a real adult with real problems.*

Since I was feeling worse than ever, I tried to be kinder to myself. I took on the tone of a nonjudgmental counselor. *Mmmm, how did that meeting make you feel?* That got me nowhere, so I went with the boot camp instructor approach: *All right, Nicole, get it together. You are in California, for goodness' sake! It's beautiful here! The sun is shining! What the heck is wrong with you?* (Scolding myself, by the way, never works.)

This is the gap between real life and the good life. I was claiming in my mind that I was now a mature adult walking in paradise while also berating myself in my soul for being so bad at merely existing. I sometimes think my brain and my heart are like a cranky old married couple, always bickering about why the dog is barking and what they should do about it. Brain told me that disappointing meetings were no big deal and I had no reason to be so upset, while Heart whined back to Brain that a whole day had been wasted, and it really was a big deal, and why would God have it be like this? Brain felt judgy and mean. Heart felt slighted and disappointed. The arguing in my head wore me out, and when I made it back to my friend's house, I headed straight to the guest bedroom, kicked off my shoes, got into bed, and pulled the covers over my head.

As I hid under the covers and closed my eyes, I sighed out a whispered *help me* prayer. "Help" prayers aren't just about God showing us the way forward with decisions. Often my help prayers are more about grounding and direction:

Help me understand me.
Help me understand why this feels the way it does.
Help me understand what this struggle is really about.

Somehow in the space of a few hours, I had gone from praising God to practically cursing Him. Oh yes, I know what it feels like to struggle over small things, to tug on a weed of frustration or insecurity or doubt, only to realize that you are actually pulling on a deep, wiry root embedded in your soul, one that goes much deeper than whatever your seemingly insignificant struggle might be.

When I woke up from that nap, an important truth was clarified, one that I wish I didn't need to keep learning. I am tempted—over and over again—to believe that a state of happiness is a direct result of God's favor. I am all about the hallelujahs when I'm happy. But because the day didn't turn out the way I planned, because I experienced the state of anything-but-happiness (regret, frustration, despair), I figured that must be a direct result of God's distance (*He doesn't care about me*) or disfavor (*He doesn't like me*). Then I wondered, *Why do such minor disappointments, such small bumps in the road, cause me such inner turmoil?* I realized my struggles that morning in California had not been one isolated event but were connected to a series of frustrations that relate to something bigger in my soul.

As I thought and prayed about this discouraging morning in the weeks that followed, I was reminded again that the little struggles are often related to something much more important: Let's call that the Struggle. The Struggle is about something much deeper than the everyday challenges. It's about the disconnect between what I believe and how I act, how I understand the promises of God and my actual experience with God. The Struggle is the frustrating place between who I want to be and who I actually am.

The Struggle Solution

The good news about the Struggle deep inside each one of us is that we don't need to resolve it on our own. In fact, as I discovered in my rounds of self-talk, that only makes things worse. Instead, we need to look outside ourselves, both for a new way to understand where we've come from and a clear way to move toward the good life we are desperately seeking. Rather than hiding or scolding or "fixing" ourselves, we need a new way to understand both the little struggles and the Struggle, and we need direction on what this good life actually looks like and the steps we can take to get there.

The book of James says, "If you don't know what you're doing, pray to the Father. He loves to help. You'll get his help, and won't be condescended to when you ask for it" (James 1:5, MSG). What I love about this promise is how certain and complete it is. It's a promise to all people, it's a promise related to everything that requires direction, and it's a promise that God will give the answer without any stipulations or requirements. God isn't going to judge you or find fault with you. He's going to give His help generously and freely and completely. That's a true and reliable promise. It means that when I have a day that goes from good to bad, when a conversation goes sideways, or when I find myself disappointed or discouraged or confused, God promises to provide what I need most—the spiritual smarts to understand what's going on and the spiritual conviction on how to move forward.

But here's the thing—God does give one requirement in the second half of the passage below. God offers to give to us freely and completely, but He also asks something of us that sounds pretty radical.

If you don't know what you're doing, pray to the
Father. He loves to help. You'll get his help, and
won't be condescended to when you ask for it. Ask

9

boldly, believingly, without a second thought. *People who "worry their prayers" are like wind-whipped waves. Don't think you're going to get anything from the Master that way*, adrift at sea, keeping all your options open.

JAMES 1:5-8, MSG (EMPHASIS ADDED)

In the second half of the passage, God asks us to surrender something that we like to hold on to very tightly—our right to doubt. We are a cynical bunch, we humans. We reserve the right to decide whether or not we want to believe in all kinds of things. We are constantly second-guessing what's worth believing in. A recent article said that more than half of Americans believe in at least one conspiracy theory—from JFK's assassination to what really happened on 9/11 to the idea that the world is flat.[1] That may seem preposterous to you, but conspiracy theories stem from the human condition of *reserving the right to not believe what we hear.* In some ways, I think we are all conspiracy theorists when it comes to God. We find ourselves doubting His intentions when the story lines don't make sense. When it comes to deciphering the world, our culture relies on logic and emotion, not on tradition or authority. Perhaps the most radical thing God could require of us is to *believe what He says.*

In the midst of our confusion, God lays down the rules of the game. He's going to give you the whole of Himself and help you figure out your true story, but you have to put something on the table too. You have to suspend your right to doubt and actually take Him at His Word.

True Reality

Dave and I have a child who practically came out of the womb screaming "*Don't believe the hype!*" I have never met a human being who finds such joy in punching holes in any plot or argument in which the reasoning doesn't make sense. He has spent the better half of his fifteen long years on an endless quest to debunk anything that is less than fully logical. Recently we began watching a TV series called *Revolution* together. The show's premise is that some nefarious force was able to extinguish all electricity from the earth. *The entire series* is built on that concept and doesn't make sense if you don't go with it.

Yet within ten minutes of the first episode of the first season, my son was plotting out all the ways the characters should have been able to harness electricity. I told him that the source of ultimate truth, Wikipedia, calls this show a "post-apocalyptic science fiction television series." I repeated multiple times: "It's fiction, honey. *Fiction.*" But he just couldn't suspend his own logic. The other morning over breakfast, he told me that he wasn't sure he could keep watching the show because the characters didn't try to use a windmill to generate power. I looked at him with a slightly crazy eye (it was early and I hadn't had coffee and I wasn't ready to *debate wind power*). I said, "Son [that's what I say when I'm about to lay down some parental wisdom and don't want anyone to talk back], you are going to need to suspend your reality if you plan to enjoy that TV show."

While the far-fetched plot of a TV program may not drive

you as crazy as it does my son, I bet there are parts of your own story that have you puzzled. We are always going to seek to understand the Struggle—it's our human nature to do so. But if the way you are doing life is just getting you to "fine," it's time for a new way. If you want to get a different result out of life than you are currently getting, you are going to have to suspend *your own understanding of reality* for a time. You've been operating with certain assumptions for a while—deep-seated beliefs about who you are and how life works. This is a normal and grown-up thing to do, but to tap into the transforming power of Christ, you must first "change and become like a child" (Matthew 18:3, CEV). In other words, this new way of life requires you to take all your assumptions about how the world works and put them aside, and to engage in a mind-shift, a heart-shift, and a will-shift toward the reality of God rather than the reality you are currently experiencing.

As you seek this understanding from God, you are not making a onetime transactional relationship with Him, in which you ask only about the areas in which you want help and receive only the answers you are looking for. It's not about dialing in the right formula so that He can dispense just the right amount of advice. God is not like a Dear Abby column. To actually seek His direction—fully, the way James describes here—will take a much more intentional approach. It will require more than just your desire and your faith—it will require your willful choice and action.

So how do we get this good life? We find it when we know what really matters in life. We find the good when we handle the four most important relationships on earth—our relationship with God, our relationship with ourselves, our relationship with others, and our relationship with the world at large—in the right way. To enter into God's way is to be willing to see all four relationships from God's perspective. It means suspending our own reality and willingly choosing to see things God's way.

In my life, much of God's view of the world stands outside of my own logic or reason. God's wisdom is like the master key that opens me up to understand all the rest of it—what matters in my life, in my choices, and in my relationships. This kind of wisdom is freeing, not confining.

Good living is the side effect of a transformed relationship with Christ. Dallas Willard says that a heart transformed by God creates people who live "in such a way that doing the words and deeds of Christ is not the focus but is a natural outcome."[2] God does the transforming, but we have an important part to play. We have power in the relationship— the power to choose. We have to want what God offers if we are going to enter into the work it takes to get there.

A Baseline Test

So is choosing to seek God's perspective on your struggles and your story worth it? I believe with all of my heart that it is. But I know that the idea of intentional action toward this vague "good life" might not be at the top of your to-do list. You might be looking for relief from a specific problem, not a general promise that God can help you through some as-yet-unnamed struggle.

So let's enter in together with the baseline test that follows—a way to find out where we are so we know if it's worth the trip to where we are going. There are ten statements that describe a person who lives the good life—using God's definition. God is quite practical about what it looks like to live as a mature and "whole" person. Every one of these statements is directly related to the way God describes the good life in His Word. I invite you to consider each statement from a completely honest place. How many describe you? There is no growth without honesty, so engage with this exercise with all the transparency you can muster.

The Good Life Inventory

Put a check by the statements that currently describe you.

_____ 1. I am totally committed to knowing the truth about myself. I am not afraid to ask others around me to help me see blind spots or trouble areas in my life.

_____ 2. I have a peaceful and nonanxious presence, both inside and out.

_____ 3. Generally I feel that my soul is untroubled and undisturbed. I have nothing to hide.

_____ 4. I regularly and sincerely ask for forgiveness from my family, friends, and coworkers.

_____ 5. I respect my own heart, body, and soul as something to be cherished.

_____ 6. I treat conflicting patterns of thinking and behaving in myself with gentleness.

_____ 7. I have a clear sense of purpose in my life.

_____ 8. I have experienced deep compassion for someone who has hurt me.

_____ 9. I feel total freedom from my past hurts and regrets.

_____ 10. I experience joy on a daily basis.

How'd it go for you . . . and how do you feel now? Even completing an inventory like this may bring up all kinds of struggles. You may feel bad about yourself. You may immediately punch holes in the logic of this questionnaire, thinking that no one is that black and white, and that life can't be reduced to a series of yes/no statements. You may think that this is all kind of dumb and trite and just another form of cheesy Christianity. I don't even need you to admit those reactions—I know them because I'm the chief cynic of us all. As much as I hate to acknowledge it, my son comes by his annoying habit of not believing the hype pretty naturally.

If you answered this inventory with honesty and humility, you likely discovered that you have a healthy perspective in some areas and work to do in others. When I posted this inventory on Facebook, I discovered that most people answer yes to between two and six statements. Regardless of your number, I bet we'd agree that the people who answer yes to all ten statements would probably be pretty great people to be around (unless they're lying or completely unaware of themselves, in which case they would be terrible to be around).

People with a peaceful presence and perspective are likely free and joyful people. Maybe you know a person like that. I hope you, like me, would also like to be that person. Knowing where we are heading begins with knowing where we are. When it comes to the good life, developing a peaceful presence begins with the self-awareness that comes from taking an honest look at how we are really doing. I love this quote from a personality theorist: "Once we understand the nature of our personality's mechanisms, we begin to have a choice about identifying with them or not. If we are not aware of them, clearly no choice is possible."[3]

The beginning of all growth is awareness. The first step is acknowledging that we may have to suspend our own understanding of reality and find a different starting point—not our own logic or emotion, but an umbrella statement of truth that will change how we view our lives.

Where We Begin

Proverbs 9:10 says that "the fear of the LORD is the beginning of wisdom." If wisdom points to the good life we're looking for, then it comes in a surprising place—the fear of the Lord! The Bible repeatedly uses the phrase "fear of the LORD." People are to learn to fear God (Deuteronomy 31:12; Psalm 34) and to know His power (Joshua 4:24). Leaders were told to work "in the fear of the LORD" in order to pursue justice (2 Chronicles 19:9). Through his deep suffering, Job discovered that "fear of the Lord—that is wisdom" (Job 28:28). The fear of the Lord leads to a full life, and is life itself (Proverbs 10:27; 14:27; 19:23). The church is strengthened and prospered when in the fear of the Lord (Acts 9:31). This phrase, which sounds foreign to our modern sensibilities, is somehow the key that moves us toward the good life. How can God be both loving and someone to be feared? Aren't those things opposed to one another? Can God fully love us and also scare us?

I once took a drive that illustrated for me what "fear of the Lord" really means. I was heading to a retreat when my navigational system directed me to make a sharp turn onto a narrow neighborhood road. I was both surprised and annoyed when Siri told me in her deep Australian accent, "For seventeen miles, continue on this route." Those seventeen miles were going to take at least an hour, and the road only got narrower and steeper as it climbed sharply up what now felt like the Alps. Never one for scenic drives, especially when I have to be somewhere, I pressed hard onto the gas pedal and leaned forward in my seat, willing my little sedan up an almost continual climb for the next few miles. Multiple thoughts demanded my attention—directions, logistics, some insecurities about how this retreat would go, my family, what was happening the following week. My mind was as busy as a six-lane highway at rush hour.

But then . . . I rounded a bend and actually gasped. As I barreled around this mountain, I got a glimpse of one of the most beautiful vistas I have ever seen. Trees stretched in every direction. The sky was piercingly blue. The ocean, hugged into a crescent by the mountains around it, lay in the distance. The city stretched out before me. *Breathtaking* is the word to describe it—as it actually took my breath away. This moment was so pure and beautiful that I could keep describing it for pages—and still not convey how striking and beautiful it was. My car kept charging forward even though I had basically vacated my job as driver, craning my neck and stretching forward in the hopes that I would catch the view again. As the road continued to climb, I caught flash after flash of this incredible view. I had places to go and a time line to keep, but the landscape demanded my attention. Suddenly nothing was as important to me as seeing that view again. At one point, I stopped my car in the middle of the road to take it in because I couldn't move on from this beauty. Its magnitude and brilliance took priority in my soul. I forgot about all the other things that had seemed important in the presence of such splendor.

When I think of the love of God and the fear of the Lord, I think of that view. My thoughts were so small when interpreted through its grandeur. The mountain's greatness commanded my attention. The fear of the Lord is natural when we acknowledge who He is and catch even a glimpse of His power and might. When I looked out at that view, all the things that people have built and created appeared tiny, eclipsed by the majesty of what God has created. Out of His great love He created great beauty:

The unfailing love of the Lord fills the earth.
The Lord merely spoke,
    and the heavens were created.
He breathed the word,
    and all the stars were born.
He assigned the sea its boundaries
    and locked the oceans in vast reservoirs.

PSALM 33:5-7, NLT

My best description of the fear of the Lord, then, is our recognition of this combination of beautiful love and majestic power.

The fear of the Lord is the acknowledgement that *God is greatest.* Things can be great—but *God is greatest.* Things can be hard—but *God is greatest.* When we interpret our challenges through that view, we get a new perspective on our struggles and desires.

The fear of the Lord makes the fact that *God is greatest* the central and starting point of every other thought we will ever have. But *God is greatest* doesn't fully capture it. If God is only greatest, He could still be a distant God. Holy and powerful—but uninvolved and unconcerned with our everyday struggles.

A fuller way of understanding His nature means we need to add to the phrase. God isn't just greatest—*He also knows best.* This is the connection between God's magnitude and His sacrificial care and wisdom. God's greatness doesn't exist in a vacuum with no effect on the smaller details of living. When we live with a dug-down-deep understanding that

God is greatest, and He knows best, we become more open to receive His direction and follow His ways. It's a natural result of believing in the fear of the Lord. Rewriting our understanding of life begins with this one phrase.

God is greatest, and He knows best.

Opening Your Heart Is a Choice

What's even more astounding about God is that He gives us freedom in how we respond to this truth. We have to make the choice to believe that God is greatest and knows best. We have to align our willpower, our logic, and our emotion behind this statement.

To continue the metaphor of my mountain drive, I didn't *have* to stop to take in this breathtaking view. I didn't even have to look at it. I could have kept my eyes on the yellow line in the center of the road and continued in the busyness of my own thoughts. In fact, my guess is that if I drove that road every day, this unbelievable view would become commonplace and easier to ignore. I would likely become blind to the wonder of it all. The view didn't make me stop and pay attention. I had to choose to do so. This is where I began to understand how easily I slip into forgetting about the greatness of God.

The greatest challenge in life will be the challenge of choice. The fact that we have the ability to make choices speaks to the freedom that God has given us to embark on a life that requires our engagement.

We not only have intentional choices to make that will directly impact our future for good, but we also have choices to make about how we react to the decisions made by others that have impacted us for evil. God can use even bitter things to create good in our lives, but all of our decisions require our intentional engagement. The way you choose to think, feel, act, and relate will have a profound effect on your story.

A Story of Choice

There's a history lesson in the Bible about the Hebrew people using their freedom to make a choice about their lives. Despite the fact that God had clearly revealed Himself to the Israelites and performed miracle after miracle to show His love and faithfulness to them, the Israelites had a tough time believing He was greatest and He knew best.

The wilderness is a harsh place. When we are in the "in-between"—between being led into freedom and actually living in that freedom—we are doubtful, fearful creatures. But this middle space is where we spend almost all of our days. And I know I'm like an Israelite when I'm in the in-between wilderness of life. Despite knowing that God is good and seeing His glory and grandeur in places like that mountain view, I forget. I struggle to remember when I'm in the wilderness, whether that looks like an unknown future or the effort to leave something difficult in my past behind.

Maybe that's why Moses had choice last words for his people before he died. After all of those years of leading them through the wilderness, encouraging and admonishing them to trust God, he had strong and important things to say. Just before they were to enter this new and free land that God had promised to them, Moses said: "This day I call the heavens and the earth as witnesses against you that I have set before you life and death, blessings and curses. Now choose life, so that you and your children may live and that you may love the LORD your God, listen to his voice, and hold fast to him. For the LORD is your life" (Deuteronomy 30:19-20).

Even though this tribe of people were living and breathing and alive, Moses reminded them that they still had *life and death* choices to make. To choose life was to choose to believe *God is greatest, and He knows best.* To choose death was to choose *I am greatest, and I know best.* It was the choice they had to make then, and it's the choice we must make now. Choosing this is not a one-and-done choice, but a continual, intentional setting of our hearts and souls to believe that life is found in God, who reveals that life through His wisdom and ultimately through Jesus Christ. We have the incredible privilege and responsibility to be active participants in our own life stories—especially in the hard, heavy, and confusing parts—in both the daily little annoyances and the big struggles related to purpose, meaning, and peace. Choosing to engage with God in our real story—*all of our story*—is the first step in experiencing life in a whole new way.

Choosing to engage with God in our real story— all of our story—is the first step in experiencing life in a whole new way.

This book, then, is an invitation to your own life. It's an invitation to *choose* life in your ordinary days, to be openhearted as you seek God's truth and refreshment in the most unlikely of places—the Struggle. The Struggle is, in fact, real. But if we can use it to lead us to God's wisdom, then our struggles—and the underlying Struggle—can be used for good.

Keeping It Real

At the end of each chapter, I offer a question, prayer, or comment for you to consider. This is an invitation to a conversation with God about the content of the chapter.

Take a look back at the Good Life Inventory and pray this simple prayer:

> Jesus, I give You all that I am—the good and the bad, the wise and the foolish, the peaceful and the anxious. I pray that You would give me courage to face who I really am and faith to accept who You really are for me. Amen.

2

The Reality

Choose Your Hard

I am obsessed with renovations, remodels, and makeovers. *I love them.* And I'm not alone—so are the millions of people who watch "transformation" reality shows every single week. From *Restaurant: Impossible* to *Fixer Upper*, we have a particular love for shows that feature redos of every kind. There are few things as satisfying as seeing a business or home that was ruined and left for dead come back to glorious life. What's even better—it happens neatly packaged into a fifty-minute show. Oh yes! I love speedy transformations that seem to turn out beautifully and end in a wow moment every time!

Can you imagine a *Fixer Upper* episode in which Chip and Joanna fail to create a beautiful renovation—or the lucky recipients fail to love it? You see, we all want a savior and we all love a savior. We may receive that saving vicariously through a broken-down restaurant or a ramshackle house that's restored to its glory. The problem is, that wow moment may quench our thirst for one hour, but then we are thirsty again.

I've felt that thirst myself, and I suspect it affects our entire generation. We don't believe the hype. Even when a part of us wants to believe in the restoration shows, another part of us is searching for clues on the Internet that perhaps one of those transformations didn't work out so we can feel a little better about what isn't changing in our own lives.

Transformation TV exists because our need for renewal and renovation is real. We all need to believe that our lives can become better, to hope that our future may be brighter despite how screwed up we feel from our past or in the present. That's a good and hopeful longing, but one that can't be met in a fifty-minute slice of our lives. For this reason, transformation TV has stolen our hope for change in two ways. One, we *stop* believing in transformation if it isn't as radical or obvious in our own stories as it is on our screens. Two, we *start* believing our lives must be too small for that kind of redemption. We forget that *our struggle is real* and that *our struggle is good.* But we don't need to stay there. Seeking more for our lives starts with one crucial question.

Choosing Real Reality

It all comes down to this: *What and who will we believe?* With so much fake reality out there, we can become jaded, believing that there's no source of objective wisdom that is consistent, real, and relevant. So I've got a proposition for you: *Choose to believe the Bible is the ultimate source of reality for your life.*

Let's be honest about how this sounds for us. At first, the Bible may seem like an unlikely place to turn for a dose of reality. I've been teaching Bible studies and doing ministry for the past twenty years, but that doesn't mean that the Bible has always been my source for how to live my life. Here's the deal: Most people don't know that much about the Bible, whether they've been around church for a long time or not. Few people read it regularly, and even if they do, they don't quite know what to do with much of it. Much of Scripture is hard to understand on the first read, and it doesn't package up like a good reality show does. I get that. I find it hard to read sometimes, too, and it takes a while to make the connection between what's happening in those pages and what's happening in my heart. Much of my time in the Bible has been about influence that's indirect and subtle, grown over time.

What's more, the Bible is definitely not reality show material. So many endings are left unwritten. So many relationships are left unmended. And so much time passes from prayers said to longings answered, from sacrifices made to blessings received, from wounds inflicted to healing completed. Yet in the midst of all of it is life—real life—the way we actually know it. Hidden within those unfinished stories is an invitation to the mystery of more, to a life lived not from fifty minutes of "whoa!" to "wow" but from moment to moment, one choice at a time. The Bible describes itself as a double-edged sword, piercing into the thoughts and attitudes of the heart (Hebrews 4:12). Theologian Peter Kreeft says that we think we are reading the Bible, while all the while, it is reading us.[1] To enter into God's story means entering into a new "reading" of our lives, one defined not just by what we can see and experience but also by what God sees and experiences in us, what God is doing around us.

Remember Moses' last words to the Israelites: "Choose life"? That wasn't just a pithy phrase of inspiration thrown out because it sounded pretty. I think Moses' "choose life" comment was a last-ditch effort to lead God's people well, to remind them that they had choices to make every day that could add up to a life well lived. It wasn't a given that just because they were God's people, all would go well for them. There was a collective identity (We are God's), and there was individual responsibility (I have a part to play).

The whole story from the Old Testament was a shadow of what was to come in Jesus. When Christ came, He was the complete fulfillment of the smaller story of the nation of Israel.

But Jesus came for a much bigger story—not just for one nation but for all nations. He came not just for one time but for our time as well—yes, for you and for me in this crazy, modern world we live in. What Jesus offered His followers is what our hearts still need now. He not only explained His Kingdom, but in His death and resurrection, He established that Kingdom right here, right now, in each of our hearts. The rest of the New Testament, from Acts through Revelation, demonstrates how life plays out with Jesus as King of the unseen but very real Kingdom of God into which we have all been invited—first on earth now, and then for eternity in heaven.

This matters because it changes *everything* about the way we interpret our stories. It means that "getting smart"— getting Jesus-smart, I mean—is a huge part of navigating our existence. To follow Jesus is a full-life conversion to a new "place." Imagine if you uprooted and replanted yourself in a new country. You would still be you, but everything around you would be different. You would learn a new language, experience a new daily rhythm, and form new relationships. When we step into Christ's Kingdom, we are transferring our hearts to a new place spiritually. Rather than uprooting and replanting our bodies, we are uprooting and replanting our spirits. If following Jesus isn't actually affecting your everyday life like this kind of move, then something is tragically amiss. I mean it. If you feel like your experience with struggles, confusion, and hardship are no different from anyone else's— whether they follow Jesus or not—something is really wrong. This is not the abundant life Jesus offered.

What I'm *not* proposing is that you need to adopt some kind of prayer or set of rules that will make your life better. A friend and leader in our church, Theresa, recently talked about her conversion to Christianity in her fifties. During the same week, both she and her husband encountered Christ and gave their lives to Him separately. When each finally told the other what had happened, they decided that they would now just become better versions of themselves. She laughed hysterically when telling me the story. "Imagine!"

she said. "We thought we would just be better versions of ourselves! Ha-ha-ha-ha!" Theresa recognizes their naiveté in believing they could be exactly the same people with a side of Jesus, rather than entirely transformed people who now live through Jesus.

If you are a transformation TV junkie like me, you need to remember that getting Jesus-smart is not going to be like a fifty-minute show that neatly ends in a "wow." The struggle is real, and it's not going away. However, it *does* mean that what is happening in you, through you, and around you—all of that is up for transformation, for change. It *does* mean that getting Jesus-smart is going to change how you do life. Theresa thinks, feels, and acts differently because of Jesus. The level of conversion—from anxiety to peace, from anger to joy, from bitterness to forgiveness—has changed her completely. But it didn't happen all at once, and it didn't necessarily come easily. But when she talks about Jesus, everything she says tells you, "This is worth it."

But—It Will Be Hard

A few years ago I grabbed a quick lunch with my friend Pete. Pete is part of the family that Dave and I stitched together as adults—the older and wiser people in our everyday lives who became our surrogate parents when we were young adults in a new city with a new marriage and new jobs and new everything. Pete is one of those guys who stuck with us even when we thought we should know everything about life, when we were little kids in grown-up bodies.

Because Pete and I serve on the same church ministry staff, we've done much of life together. Pete and I have gotten frustrated with each other, we've cried about things, we've apologized. Pete was there to visit when Dave and I had each of our children. I went to see him in the hospital when he had his knee replaced. Once you've seen each other in a hospital bed, you are basically family. And those people who loved you in your inflated, self-important early adulthood years—who loved you then and still love you now—well, they are priceless.

During that lunch over bad fast-food salads, Pete and I caught up about the happenings in our lives. Me—in the square middle of it, middle childhood with the kids, middle management in my work, middle of figuring out what ministry was supposed to look like, how to live with purpose and passion and do this "life" thing. He—rounding the finish line in almost all of those ways, and also figuring out what ministry was supposed to look like in the unknown beyond of the empty nest. And then right in the middle of it all, right in the middle of the ordinary stuff of everyday conflict and frustration and the worries and the unknown, Pete put down his fork. I don't remember what we were talking about before this moment, but I'll never forget what happened next.

Pete stopped chatting and looked at me intently, and then he teared up. My chicken stuck in my throat a little as he paused for a moment, took a deep breath, and said, "You will suffer." He looked at me again, and I felt as if he were looking past me into a deeper place, and I was getting uncomfortable.

He nodded his head slowly and said, "There is suffering coming in this. You will not grow without it."

I shrugged my shoulders and laughed it off. Then I changed the topic because whatever he was seeing right then—whatever Jesus-smart thing he could see that I couldn't—I didn't want to know about it, I didn't want it to be true. I felt as if my life was too good to even use the word *suffer*. I felt like I wasn't old enough for that; not to mention that I still thought I could escape from that word and that world, that somehow I could struggle but not suffer.

I was wrong.

If you are like me, most of your life involves struggle. We struggle to keep up with our schedules and to fit in our workouts and to eat enough fiber. We struggle to hold our tongues when we want to snap, and we struggle to find the blessing when we want to complain. The struggle is, in fact, real. But sometimes—and for all of us, this time will come—well, sometimes we suffer.

The word *suffering* has this torturous quality to it. We often think it should be reserved for the worst of circumstances—for painful, incurable diseases; for tragic and evil death; for famine and war. *Surely* we wouldn't refer to the everyday struggles in our stories that way. But I think we lose when we don't acknowledge the simple reality that we suffer. Sometimes what was an annoying struggle becomes a painful, long season of disappointment. Perhaps the easiest way to define suffering is a struggle of any kind that isn't resolved and doesn't go away—at least not in your way or on your timetable. Your suffering will probably not look like famine or war. Maybe it'll look more like an aching loneliness or an unspoken longing. Maybe it will look like a thorny relationship that keeps getting sharper. Your suffering might look like a season of gray, a deep fog that settles over your soul. It might look like a long season of disappointment— where the present is boring and the future is bleak. It might look like the stony face of your teenager, that same face you once cupped in your hands but whose generous, loving spirit seems to have vacated his body. Using the word *suffering* for our lives isn't giving ourselves an excuse, or at least it doesn't have to be. *Instead, naming our reality for what it is, whether struggle or suffering, is the beginning of seeing the whole of our spiritual story.*

In 2 Corinthians, comfort and suffering are closely linked. God—the "God of all comfort" (1:3)—will comfort us in our troubles, and then we are called to comfort others in their troubles. All of that makes sense and feels right, but the passage goes on to say that "we share abundantly in the sufferings of Christ" (1:5).

If I could talk to Paul in person, I would stop him and say, "Wait a second, buddy. Hold it right there. You seem to indicate that suffering is a *given.*" Since I feel like Paul might be a guy who likes to shoot straight, I imagine he might say something like, "Um, yes, what life have you been living? Of course it's a given!" This is Paul, who goes on in this letter to talk about all of the hardships he's suffered, of despairing even of his life.

We can ignore the struggle or avoid it. We can downplay it or hide it. We can blame someone else for it. But we will never grow through it if we do not own it as our story in its fullest, rawest, realest form. The struggle is hard and painful. Suffering is even worse. But what the Bible says about the suffering is very different from what transformation TV portrays. God says that although the struggle may be hard, that doesn't mean it's bad. Suffering can be hard *and* good. Struggles can be painful *and* fruitful. Life is lived in the gray space between the two.

Suffering can be hard and good. Struggles can be painful and fruitful. Life is lived in the gray space between the two.

Paul loves to clarify the role of suffering in our faith. He frequently makes the connection between struggle and growth. Romans 5 calls us to not only survive our struggles, but to celebrate them: "We can rejoice, too, when we run into problems and trials, for we know that they help us develop endurance. And endurance develops strength of character, and character strengthens our confident hope of salvation. And this hope will not lead to disappointment" (Romans 5:3-5, NLT).

What's amazing about this promise is that it tells us struggles are going to do the exact opposite of what we expect. Our struggles always seem to lead to disappointment—but in Christ, those same struggles cultivate endurance, strength, and hope.

I sometimes wonder if we can experience deep transformation without struggle. To be honest, I wish we could, but my experience with people shows me that the deeper the struggle, the deeper the person. When we deal with the painful realities in our lives, something happens in us that doesn't seem possible without the pain. I don't like that it's true, but that doesn't make it less true. In the mystery of God's wisdom, He uses struggles and sometimes suffering to clarify exactly who we are and who He created us to be. Through our suffering, He also demonstrates that He is exactly who He claims to be throughout Scripture: "our refuge and strength, an ever-present help in trouble" (Psalm 46:1).

Struggles are not fun. They are not glamorous. They are not easy. But that doesn't make them *not* good. From cover to cover, the Bible is open about our raw reality in the struggle. It's about the beautiful results created from the struggle. It's about the intangible and eternal things learned in the struggle, and it's about the people we can become through the struggle. The story line that we've bought about life—the one that says if it's not easy, it's not good—is a lie. Over time, it's a hard lie to keep up. It leaves us always feeling disappointed or resentful. We secretly believe our particular circumstances are harder than we deserve, but outwardly, we pretend we are too spiritual to get worked up about them. Our struggles are somehow too big for us and too small for God.

But our struggles are the training ground for wisdom. What matters most are not the circumstances we face, but what we will do with them, what we will learn from them, what we will do after we get into and out of one ditch and hike toward the next. Difficult circumstances always demand attention. The question is, what kind of attention will we give them? One option is to expend a ton of energy to hide, cover, and react to them. The other—and

I promise, better choice—is simply to face them head-on with a whole different perspective.

One of my young friends just came out of a bad relationship. (Can I get an amen from all the readers out there who are trying to love their "bad relationship" friend?) The amount of emotional energy she expended on this guy could have powered all the sadness of a small country. Every conversation between them was loaded; every text was a secret message that must mean something different. Despite the fact that the guy mostly seemed like a jerk, my friend continued to try to translate the meaning of every encounter to keep the relationship alive. At one point, I gently pointed out that sometimes relationship resuscitation doesn't work and that perhaps it was time to back away from the body. But she wasn't ready for that.

Struggles are the training ground for wisdom.

Looking back, I think the relationship was really hard for her, but facing reality was just a little bit harder. It took a few months and a lot of hard knocks to her heart, but she was eventually able to choose honesty. She was able to see that actions speak louder than words, and that it was time to let the boyfriend go. The choices on the table were to choose hard or choose harder. Choosing easy wasn't even an alternative.

Now let's consider our own lives. I think we want to believe that "choosing easy" is always on the menu. We hope that "easy" must be the next course, and we will just kind of push the food around in whatever course we are living and wait for the delicious next round. But that's not reality. To choose wisdom is the harder choice—because it starts with facing reality. It takes honesty with ourselves and with others. When we choose honesty, we see things in ourselves that we really don't like. When we choose honesty, we realize the places we struggle and the places where we may have to suffer. But the choice we must make is how we will *see* the hard. Strangely and sometimes unbelievably, it's actually in our trials that we experience real joy and freedom. In a crazy twist of reality, facing all that is hard and messy leads to freedom.

The book of James opens with these words, "Consider it pure joy, my brothers and sisters, whenever you face trials of many kinds" (James 1:2). James goes on to connect the trials we face with the perseverance of our faith. And what makes our faith grow? The wisdom God provides in the midst of those struggles. So rather than avoiding them, downplaying them, or outsourcing them to other people, what if we decided that choosing hard in the midst of our struggles is choosing reality?

The struggle can never be real if we don't get real about the struggle. But struggles are a "pay now or pay later" type of situation. We can pay now—we can do the hard work in the moment, as it's happening. Or we can pay later. We can let all the suffering and hurt start to pile up, weighing down our souls. We can hang on and hope for the best and keep trying harder. But eventually, the weight will crack us, and it will break us. But praise be to God who offers us healing repeatedly, persistently, and thoroughly.

Home Base

When Pete interrupted my mediocre lunch and life with the jarring pronouncement that I would suffer, he was right. In the year that followed, I suffered. It wasn't public. I didn't experience sudden and tragic death. My husband didn't lose his job; our marriage didn't fall apart. None of my kids were given a diagnosis or suffered a trauma. Everything I would consider "big" enough for suffering—none of that happened. But turbulence came. I had a recurring nightmare that made me wake up sweating. I saw relationships that were cracking begin to completely fracture. I experienced a deep, thick layer of disappointment around a dream. I felt betrayed and abandoned by those who had loved me before. All of it happened quietly and privately.

Because no one circumstance felt like a life-changing, horrible event, I tried to rationalize each one away and soldier on by ignoring how I really felt about what was going on around me. Despite my love of honesty, I had a hard time being truthful with myself. I didn't want to use the *suffering* word for my pretty-good life. I didn't think I could own a word so big, so spiritual, a word that seemed to be much more dramatic than the issues I was facing.

But I've come to look back on that season and see that what was happening quietly was death—deaths of all kinds. Along with some of my dreams and relationships dying, some of my idealism was killed off, along with a healthy dose of unrealistic expectations. The part of me that loves transformation TV began to see these shows for what they are—a brief respite from reality, not reality itself. All the thin veneers of "fine" living that I had painted over the pain began to peel off, slowly, and with the peeling back, layers of my own heart seemed to peel away too. I discovered I was much less in control and much weaker than I wanted to believe. I found myself more anxious about everything—getting older, parenting, feeling valuable at work, and handling conflict in my relationships. I was navigating the inevitable losses of life with a lot less panache than I expected from myself.

The struggles, at least day by day, feel controllable. The suffering feels bigger and scarier. I didn't want the suffering, and in that, I was avoiding the two big truths we've discovered so far: Following God is worth it, and seeing the Bible as our ultimate reality makes our path much clearer. I finally ran out of my own strength, my own ideas, and my own ability to live in this uncomfortable and personal darkness. And when I would wake up in the middle of the night again, when I would lie in bed with my eyes wide open, willing myself to see physically but knowing that only spiritual eyes would give me vision, I began to say "help." I prayed "help me" again, my fuller, more wordy prayers giving way to a simple and desperate and honest ask, over and over again. I prayed "help" like I really needed it. This was not a *Can you give me a hand with the groceries?* kind of help. This was the *rescue me* kind of help, the desperate help. It was the most honest thing that came out of me through that whole season. And then one night, while praying with my whole heart, feeling my heart crying *help*,

I felt a phrase impressed on my heart, like a note still warm from folding being slipped into my hand. The phrase was simple: *Return to home base.*

I'm no baseball player. I have a hard time even watching the game (I'm always there for the socializing). But I knew what home base meant. Home base was safe. Home base was what we called the place of security when we played an elaborate game of tag growing up. To get back to home base was to be in the safe zone. And although it was a small area, within that space I always felt totally free. I turned the phrase over in my mind, considering the ultimate home base, the promise I knew to be true:

God is greatest, and He knows best.

As those days pressed on me, when I felt like I couldn't summon the strength to handle all the needs around me, I reminded myself that *God is greatest.* His ways are highest. He is never surprised. He could navigate my inner world far better than I ever could. "Search me, God, and know my heart; test me and know my anxious thoughts." Those words from Psalm 139:23 became a well-worn prayer, but I began to pray that verse more honestly and added the next verse as well: ". . . lead me in the way everlasting." Now I wanted God to not just search me, not just know me, but also guide me. Lead me into the way for the singular day ahead, the singular choice ahead.

God is greatest, and He knows best.

In the midst of that suffering season, that only-choice-is-surrender season, I learned that we don't gain God's wisdom in the "wow" moments. The kind of wisdom gained in hardship comes from ruthless honesty before God—a deeper searching. It's about a desperate desire to be known and to be given just enough faith to be led. This deeper searching often means tracing our stories back to discover pockets of hurt or unforgiveness or deception that require Jesus' healing and truth. Sometimes the struggle means we have to double back down a path we thought we had already covered, to retrace some old steps, to find important treasure that we left behind in that last scuffle.

That suffering season taught me that we all need a home base to return to, and from that home base, we make small, faithful choices. Then we "choose life" in the way we honor our bodies, our minds, and our hearts through the daily care and keeping of our souls. During another hard season recently, it seemed like the smallest daily choices were the ones that broke me free. First, I decided to be completely honest before God, using uncensored, unfiltered, and often irrational words when talking with Him. When I prayed, "I don't want this" and "This isn't fair" and "Where are You?" I realized I was allowing my soul space to vent before resting in the truth that *God is greatest, and He knows best.* And although this may sound a little weird, my second small choice was to eat an apple every day. Eating an apple became a tangible reminder that I needed to take care of myself, that it was worth taking the time to cut an apple *just for me,* and that this one tiny choice was one healthy step in the right direction.

You see, the most real place of struggle is not on the outside, where others can see it. The struggle is most real on the inside, in the inner places. We bring those inner places before God with the most uncut and specific reality, and then we make those small outer choices that honor our souls. Ann Voskamp says in her book *The Broken Way*: "Busy is a choice. Stress is a choice. Giving yourself to joy is a choice. Choose well."[2]

A few months ago, I spoke with my prophetic friend Pete again. I put my hand on his arm and told him I remembered that day when he promised me suffering. And this time I was the one who teared up when I said, "You were right." And I did two things at once: I clenched my jaw together and I smiled. Both were genuine. Choosing the hard is like that. It's a clench-your-jaw and get set for reality with a break-free smile of freedom and joy.

When we find our way to reality, when we kick through our own defenses and get to the raw honesty, we make an incredible discovery. Jesus is already there, catching us at the bottom, welcoming us to the way of freedom, leading us forward, one small, wise choice at a time. Choosing our hard reality often means going back before we can go forward. Choosing reality is asking the simple question, *God, what do I need to know?* It's praying the simple prayer: *God, what do You want to heal?* When we face reality square on, we let God begin the process of rewriting the story.

Keeping It Real

1. Have you experienced good struggle? If yes, what did you learn from it?

2. Think about your own story. Has it been easier for you to acknowledge struggles as important or to acknowledge suffering as real?

3. What's one small, wise choice you can make to care for your body, your mind, or your heart this week? (Think really small. Don't forget the apple story. Change takes time and requires small victories.)

The Truth
Who We Really Are

The color of truth is grey.

ANDRÉ GIDE

The day finally came. After months of pleading, reasoning, bargaining, and swearing that I was old enough, that it was worth it, that it was time, I'd worn my mom down at last.

I was getting a perm.

Now, dear reader, for those of you who did not have the distinct honor to live through the perm era, or on whom God has bestowed the special favor of having naturally curly hair, you may not understand the overwhelming hopefulness that bubbled in me that morning, the *morning of the perm.* Everyone who was anyone had a perm. Perms spanned every personality. Carol on *Growing Pains* had a perm, and she was uptight. Jennifer on *Family Ties* had a perm, and she was a tomboy. Screech from *Saved by the Bell* had a perm—and he was an actual boy! After suffering for many months with a too-short haircut that had people in the grocery store asking if my brother and I were twins (as in, *two little boys*), I was ready for my perm to transform me into the beautiful, popular preteen I knew I had the potential to become when I got the hair right.

We pulled up to my mom's friend's house, who assured my mom she was basically a hairstylist. This should have been my first red flag. If someone told me they were "basically" a surgeon, I would not have them remove an organ. Beauticians go to school for a reason, people. But we didn't have a lot of money growing up, so I took what I could get. My own funding stream was limited to the two neighbors' houses I could walk to for babysitting gigs, so I wasn't exactly rolling in my own cash.

The "beautician" piled us all into the hall bathroom, where I perched on the toilet seat while my mom's friend pulled and smoothed my locks into brightly colored rollers and squirted the chemical solution onto my scalp, the fumes burning my nose hairs. I had some time to think while the "perm" took, and I remember smiling at myself from the toilet seat, imagining my new post-perm life. Although the whole atmosphere was not quite the spa-salon experience I'd envisioned, my enthusiasm could not be flagged. *I was getting a perm.*

The time came for the rollers to be removed, my hair rinsed, and my new image revealed. The rest is a bit of a blur. I remember toweling off and looking at my hair in the mirror. I was shocked that I looked exactly like the girl who had come into the bathroom/salon/perm fun house, except with hair that was so tightly curled it resembled miniature Slinkys all over my head. My face was the face of a preteen; my hair was the hair of Blanche from *The Golden Girls*. I remember the ride home, stunned that my transformation was not girlish to glamorous, but more like somewhat awkward to downright tragic. Here is how my stages of hair grief unfurled (pun intended):

Stage 1: Denial. Drove home in silence, sure that the curls just needed a few hours to relax and bounce into perfect-perm shape. Held stubbornly on to hope that I would soon be transformed into one of my television icons.

Stage 2: Anger. As hours passed, the permanence of the perm began to set in (literally). My anger turned outward. How could I subject the precious little hair I had to an at-home perm?

Stage 3: Bargaining. I prayed. I brushed. I washed. I conditioned. But the curls refused to budge. It was as if every strand on my head was finally able to express itself fully and gloriously into a tightly spiraled cap of curls that would make Bozo jealous. My curls had the strength to resist all attempts to change them. If a fly landed in my hair, it would have been trapped. I could hold a whole set of pens between those curls, and maybe a stapler too.

Stage 4: Depression. My mood darkened. My hopes sank. There's a reason they call it a perm. *The perm was permanent.*

Stage 5: Acceptance. This is the final stage of grief, but I never made it there. My hair was too short, and the perm was too at-home to ever be what I had expected it to be.

When I showed up at school the next day with my curl-cap of hair, it was worse than I could have imagined. As we lined up for class that morning (and every morning after that), a boy named Doug would make sure he was positioned next to me, where he landed a barrage of insults, his favorite being the simple and effective, "Clown!" Probably because I had no idea how to be cool when someone teased me, I reacted. I shot back with insults, which only egged him on. No matter that he had a mullet—in the world of 1980s junior high, he had the weapons and I was his hostage. I tried to ignore him and pretend what he said didn't matter, but he was relentless. I was hurt and ashamed, and I was miserable. I expended enormous energy trying to keep the tears from falling out of my eyes while I waited for what felt like an excruciatingly long time at the classroom door, desperate to escape to the relative safety of the classroom.

I didn't tell my parents about it. I still don't know why, except that maybe I thought the best way to deal with it was to pretend it didn't happen. And it was my fault, right? After all, I was the one who wanted the perm. I would have to live with it.

Several months later, we moved across the country. The perm had relaxed into a frizzy bob that I could at least pull back in a clip, and I was able to leave that terrible chapter behind. I had been ridiculed and singled out brutally for months, and now I planned to slam that door in my heart shut and never speak of it again.

Defining Moments

I think we often expect the hallmark moments in life to be the defining ones—first days of school and graduations and weddings. It's easy to believe that the most important parts of our stories happen on the biggest days. And of course, those big days are unforgettable, but what if the main substance of what makes you *you* is found in other moments? The unseen moments. The moments when an opportunity comes and we act, or react, in ways that reveal the true nature of our hearts and our souls.

I thought that I had buried the hurt and shame following the Perm Incident, but what remained was the visceral reaction I had whenever I perceived a moment of weakness. Well into adulthood, whenever I felt uncertain or embarrassed, I went on the defensive, afraid someone would use my weakness against me. The Perm Incident and its aftermath were integral to the story I told myself about my life for many years.

How about you? Maybe it's a moment in your twenties that reminded you of a hardship in your teens. Or maybe a moment in your forties that revealed the substance of who you had become. These are the moments that shape the stories of our lives—the stories we ourselves believe about the lives we've been given.

Psychologists have studied this tendency in humans to describe our lives in a story.[1] This understanding of our development as people theorizes that we interpret ourselves as *actors*, *agents*, and *authors* of our lives.

The actor is the part of ourselves that developed when we were children and began to interpret the world around us and discover what roles we played—how the world around us viewed our temperaments and our traits, and reacted to who we were. Acting and reacting to the responses we received from our family, caregivers, and siblings, we began to play that role, for better or for worse. Our role as a child might have been "outgoing" or "fearful" or "smart." The roles we play expand as we grow up, and we take on new roles as "mom" or "teacher" or "anxious." These roles are integrated into our understanding of ourselves.

The agent is the part of ourselves that has the capacity to set goals and move toward them. Whereas the actor part of us has to live with the traits we've been given, the agent asks, *Who do I want to become?* and then plans how to get there. The agent is the empowered part of ourselves that wants to shape our desired future.

The final layer of self is the author, the capacity we have to see our lives as a story. The author integrates moments of life into a narrative arc, "the many different scenes that comprise a story, extending back to the past and forward to the future."[2] Studies have shown that the way people articulate the story of their lives has a great impact on their overall well-being. In one study, those who had the highest satisfaction with life and deepest commitment to others told their life story in a redemptive arc. They were able to integrate episodes of struggle and hardship into a story that reflected a sense of ultimately overcoming and learning from the struggle.

Apparently, the moments we remember and the stories we tell about our parts in the stories—actor, agent, author—really do matter. Here's a simple way to express this truth:

Who We Are + Moments That Matter = Stories We Live

Our choices and actions flow from the way we understand ourselves on the grand stage of life, how we decide what moments matter, how we tell our own story to ourselves, and how we live because of it.

Finding Our Story

Psychologists may give us a framework to understand the way we see ourselves, but if I can't actually see my life differently—if I'm stuck in the actor, agent, author self I've created apart from God—I will always end up feeling like I'm not enough. So how do we each discover our story? Finding our story means engaging with honesty about the forces that have shaped us into who we are—our big and little struggles, our understanding of who we are and how we fit into the world, and most importantly, how we understand ourselves in relationship with God. God is ultimate truth and reality, and without Him, we won't find security in the midst of our struggles or freedom despite our failures. This is where God's gift of His Word makes all the difference. In chapter 2, I proposed that in order to pursue real wisdom, in order to get Jesus-smart, we need to *see the Bible as ultimate reality*. And in God's creative and gracious way, He gives us stories in the Bible that help us interpret our story. The stories in Scripture are gritty, funny, poignant, unfinished, and real. So are we. And when we see the entirety of His Word as our ultimate reality, we find the main plot of our own story.

Two dudes and a wise woman

Take, for example, the story in the Old Testament of a foolish guy, an impulsive leader, and a wise woman. It's a story within a story, a defining moment within the longer unfolding story of the life of David, a main player in Scripture who was specially called by God to be the king of Israel. Scripture describes David as a "man after [God's] own heart" (1 Samuel 13:14). If you know his whole life story (told in 1 and 2 Samuel and 1 and 2 Chronicles), you realize that David's life and actions didn't always follow the course we would expect for the guy who had God's heart. But this is where the beauty of God's story comes to life. The chapters aren't clean, clear, and straightforward. God's people wander and struggle—just like us. But when we take a closer look, we discover what it means to coauthor our stories with God at the center.

We pick up this story in 1 Samuel 25, which is set during a low point in David's life. Anointed by the prophet Samuel as a young teenager, David had now waited fifteen years to come into the fullness of his leadership. The "actor" self of David had an important role to play as king of Israel, God's chosen. The "agent" self—the part in David driven to set goals and meet them—well, that David was frustrated. On the run from the current king, Saul, David wandered in the desert of Judea, jumping into skirmishes here and there, leading his own disgruntled band of followers. (How's this for a résumé? In describing David's men, 1 Samuel 22:2 says, "All those who were in distress or in debt or discontented gathered around him.") This must not have been the story David imagined when he was declared the future king.

To make matters worse, the prophet Samuel had just

died. The one man who had been a visible reminder to David that what God had promised would come to pass was gone. I imagine that David was anxious and insecure. I wonder what lines of poetry David wrote looking up at the desert sky, what prayers of petition he whispered. I think he worried. I think he wondered if he had gotten his story wrong.

In his effort to stay the course, to stay faithful to God's promise to him, and to trust God's timing, David wanted to lead his men well. As they wandered through the desert, David and his men used their might to protect the shepherds and flocks of a rich man named Nabal. In those days, you couldn't call your neighborhood watch if something was going wrong on your cul-de-sac. This was a time of conquest, when "stronger takes from weaker" ruled the day. It would be quite common for a sheep or two (or a worker or two) to be stolen or mistreated in the desert by bands of thieves or neighboring tribes. But David and his men were like the Robin Hood of the Bible. Instead of stealing from Nabal, David's guys had made sure that the rich man's workers were safe and cared for in the wilderness, a fact corroborated by Nabal's own men (see 1 Samuel 25:15-16).

When sheep-shearing time, a festive occasion for those tending flocks, rolled around, David instructed his men to approach the wealthy landowner to ask for some provisions for a celebration of their own. After all, they had ensured the safety of Nabal's sheep. But when David's men made their request, Nabal told a very different story about what had happened. He responded with a sneer and an insult: "Who is this David?" (verse 10).

Nabal attacked David's identity.

Nabal then called David a fugitive from the current king, Saul. Nabal added to the insult: "Many servants are breaking away from their masters these days" (verse 10).

Nabal attacked David's personal history.

"Why should I take *my* bread and water . . . and give it to men coming from who knows where?" (verse 11, emphasis added).

Nabal revealed his own story about how life works.

In this batch of put-downs, Nabal refused to follow traditional forms of hospitality to David's men. He returned their good with his own selfishness. He used the pronoun *I* or *me* four times in his response. Clearly, Nabal was the star character in the story he was writing about his life. Nabal's sense of self can be summarized like this:

I'm the main player in my own story.

I'm the one who makes it all happen.

I'm responsible for my success, and I'm the one who reaps the benefits.

So how would David, "God's guy," handle this turn of events? Pop quiz! When David's men reported Nabal's rebuff, David, the "man after [God's] own heart," responded by:

a. going off by himself to ask for God's help

b. moving out of that part of the desert to find a party elsewhere

c. strapping on his sword and vowing to kill everyone

Ding ding ding! If you guessed c, you are absolutely correct. Yes, David, the man after God's heart, the man of poetry and wisdom, responded to an insult from this inconsequential guy with nothing short of a war cry. And David backed up his threat with a vow: "May God deal with David, be it ever so severely, if by morning I leave alive one male of all who belong to him!" (1 Samuel 25:22). David actually invoked a curse upon himself should he not deal swiftly with Nabal.

Side note: Does David's fury feel like a literal case of overkill to anyone else? Of course, we must understand that ancient Judah was very different from our modern culture, but even so, David does respond impetuously to this insult. Obviously, his violent response is not just about Nabal, a man he's never met. I think David's response was much more about the story he was living—the wondering and waiting to become king; living on the run from Saul, who was bent on murdering him; and leading and providing for his surly band of followers. And now this—Nabal's assault on his identity, his history, and his leadership.

David was thirsty for revenge and so, apparently, were his men. They were itching to fight Nabal, the fool. But Proverbs 26:4 warns, "Do not answer a fool according to his folly, or you yourself will be just like him." My version of that proverb: If you answer a fool like Nabal with foolishness, now you have two fools.

With swords strapped on, David's four hundred men marched out for the fight. David was ready to answer Nabal's craziness with a little crazy of his own, and the result would be inevitable bloodshed, death, and continued animosity. Not exactly a pretty picture.

But just when the story looked as if it would end like a bad war movie, enter Abigail, Nabal's wife. Why would someone described as "intelligent and beautiful" (1 Samuel 25:3) be married to a fool like Nabal? Perhaps she was given to Nabal in an arranged marriage. Most likely there was little interaction before marriage, so perhaps she didn't know (or didn't have a say in) what kind of man she would wed. Or maybe Nabal's growing wealth had made him prideful and selfish. Like many of our stories, it's complicated. But unlike many of us, Abigail didn't allow her circumstances to corrupt her character. In fact, perhaps those very struggles strengthened her for the moment in front of her.

After overhearing the interchange between Nabal and David's men, some of Nabal's servants immediately reported to Abigail what had happened. "Think it over and see what you can do, because disaster is hanging over our master and his whole household" (verse 17).

"Abigail wasted no time" (verse 18, NLT). (What enterprising woman ever wastes time?) She packed a picnic fit for a king. Hundreds of loaves of bread, five sheep ready for roasting, plus raisins and dried figs. This girl was *prepared.* She sent her servants ahead of her, donkeys loaded down with gift after gift—and she set out on a dangerous mission to meet the hundreds of men looking for a fight.

Can you imagine what it must have looked like to David's men as this parade of food moved toward them? They were already armed for battle and ready to go. For Abigail to walk out of the safety of her community was to risk her own life. She literally stepped out in faith!

When she met David, she treated him 100 percent differently from the way Nabal had treated him. Bowing low to the ground, she called herself David's "servant" (verses 24 and 27), a sign of her respect for his leadership and reputation. And she didn't stop there.

Abigail called out David's true identity: "Please forgive your servant's presumption. The LORD your God will certainly make a lasting dynasty for my lord, because you fight the LORD's battles" (verse 28).

Abigail called out David's real history: "The life of my lord will be bound securely in the bundle of the living by the LORD your God" (verse 29).

Abigail called out the best story in David: As she pleaded with him not to carry out his plans, Abigail said, "When the LORD has fulfilled for my lord every good thing he promised . . . my lord will not have on his conscience the staggering burden of needless bloodshed" (verses 30-31).

In an incredible act of shrewdness, Abigail reminded David of his identity—as the future king of Israel. She reminded him of his real history—as the young warrior who conquered the giant Goliath with just five stones and a sling. She reminded David of his true story—as God's anointed. She risked her own life to remind him of his best story—one in which the future king trusted God to avenge his enemies rather than taking on the battle himself.

In the presence of this humble, beautiful, risk-taking woman bowing before him, David finally demonstrated why he was called a man after God's own heart. Despite having made an impulsive vow to kill all of Nabal's men, David listened to Abigail (who, by the way, certainly wasn't afraid to speak—her monologue lasts eight verses!). When reminded of his true identity, David relented. When reminded of God's faithfulness, David repented. When used in the New Testament, the word for "repent," *metanoia,* means "change of heart." And that is exactly what happened to David in the presence of Abigail's wisdom and grace. When she reminded him of his true story, David declared: "Praise be the LORD, the God of Israel, who has sent you today to meet me" (verse 32). In the presence of wisdom, David remembered and *chose* the best story. He didn't have to change his mind, but in his humility, David remembered who he was and what the best story of his life really meant. David accepted Abigail's gift and sent her home in peace.

In her bold and wise action, Abigail not only preserved her own household, she saved David from reactive foolishness that he would surely have regretted. That was one wise woman.

Can you imagine the relief that must have flooded through Abigail as she watched David's men fade back into the desert? Can you imagine the strength drying up, the resolve weakening, the knees sagging? I wonder if she allowed herself a moment to breathe or to shed a few tears. I wonder if she whispered a prayer of thanksgiving to God as she turned back home, now empty-handed. I wonder if the servants were immediately bubbling over with words, or if they were silent in the presence of their mistress's strength. What we do know is that Abigail turned to head home to the foolish man she had to live with, the man whose life she'd just saved, the man who had no idea what lengths she had pursued to cover up his foolishness with wisdom.

Now, friends, what do you think Abigail did when she saw her foolish husband? I'm sure none of you can relate to the feeling of "I told you so." I'm sure none of you have ever been in a contentious relationship where you were proven right and had the sweet deliciousness of being able to let your opponent know. I'm sure you've never had an argument that you couldn't wait to win. Of course, being the meek and mild woman that I am with my sweet baby-doll groom, I couldn't relate. My husband and I *never* try to prove each other wrong. I certainly would *never* march home from work to announce that I did, in fact, discover that I was right about some little thing that we had gone back and forth about that morning. No, dear reader, I have no idea what it's like to want to be so right that it hurts. (Sarcasm alert, in case it isn't dripping off this page.)

But this is not what wise women do. Abigail proceeded home, where Nabal was "holding a banquet like that of a king" (verse 36). The irony of this moment is not lost on us. Abigail had just been in the presence of royalty—the future king of Israel. Now she'd returned home to her own story— to a foolish man whose selfishness had almost gotten him and everyone else killed, who was now reveling like royalty. He may have had the temporary trappings of a king, but he had none of the character. Abigail found him "in high spirits and very drunk" (verse 36).

Quiz time! How did this fool's wife handle this moment? She responded by:

a. confronting Nabal in front of the party about what had just happened
b. packing her bags to leave her husband while everyone was distracted
c. acting like everything was fine, holding her tongue until the next morning

You guessed it, my friends. Abigail not only had the wisdom to speak boldly to David about his better story, she also had the self-control not to speak when the time wasn't right. Oh, friends, I could use more Abigail in my life! So often I feel tongue-tied in moments that require bold faith and loose-lipped in moments when I need to shut up. But not Abigail. She had the power to choose her words—and the timing of them—wisely.

So she said nothing until the following morning. Once the revelry of the night before had worn off and Nabal was sober, Abigail told him everything.

And in the harsh light of reality and the incredible turn of events, Nabal's "heart failed him and he became like a stone." Ten days later, Scripture reports, "The LORD struck Nabal and he died" (verses 37-38).

When David heard about Nabal's death, he immediately sent word to Abigail, asking her to become his wife. I know, I know—crazy! This was certainly a different day and time. Perhaps David had been instantly attracted to Abigail's beauty and intelligence. Maybe he knew it was a good move to acquire Nabal's land and household. Most likely, it was a little of both. What we do know is that Abigail's wisdom led to a better story, for her, for her entire household, and for David.

Fairy tale, right? Is this where the Bible feels more fiction than fact? Well, it's true that parts of this narrative do feel like a Cinderella story. It does seem to have a fairy-tale ending . . . or does it? The narrative closes with this gem: "David had also married Ahinoam of Jezreel" (verse 43). Out of nowhere, we get this little truth bomb dropped on the story. This was no Cinderella ending, and David was no prince. Yes, he was the future king of Israel, and yes, he wrote most of the Psalms, and yes, he was God's anointed—but he was far from perfect. Polygamy was not God's design, but it had developed over the generations as a culturally acceptable arrangement. We may not know what it was really like to be in that household, but we do know what it's like to be human. We know what it's like to compare ourselves, to be insecure, to be envious. And in the sweep of biblical history, having multiple wives never ends well—including for David.

This was not a fairy-tale ending. This was a gritty story involving real people—who made courageous decisions and big mistakes, who faced moments of choice when their character was tested and revealed. This is also a story that is left unfinished. After this narrative, we hear little about Abigail. We know she mothered David's second child (2 Samuel 3:3). We know she saw David become king (2 Samuel 2:4), but beyond that, we don't know how her story turned out or what struggles she faced later in life. What we do know is that Abigail, with her courage, resourcefulness, and humility, is one of the most powerful examples of wisdom in the Bible.

You and I may never face down a band of mountain men bent on killing our husbands and households. I can safely say you and I will never pack up a donkey load of butchered sheep and fig cakes as peace offerings to make up for the actions of our foolish husbands. But you and I will face moments of opportunity when we have choices to make for the good not only of ourselves, but of the people we love. We will have moments when we must choose the stories we believe and act upon. So how do we take this ancient story of intelligence and intrigue and pull it into our own time? We know that Nabal, David, and Abigail all believed a story about themselves. So let's distill the lessons for us.

Truth #1: Attitude leads to action.

Oxford defines *attitude* as "a settled way of thinking or feeling about something."[3] The simple but strong truth of this story, and of our own lives, is that we settle into a mode of thinking and feeling that will determine our actions moving forward. What most of us don't realize is that the *settled* way we think and feel is the result of how we write the story of our lives—the way we interpret our experiences, particularly difficult ones.

My terrible perm was not a damaging experience because my reputation for fashion took a hit (although I think my hair was damaged for at least a decade). The terrible perm was damaging because of how it shook my understanding of my roles and goals. Up to that point, I had a sense that I could make plans that would help me play my ideal role in life. I believed that I could set and reach a goal that would bring me the happiness I wanted. But the bad perm and the subsequent bullying forced a rewrite of that story. The bad perm was my first experience in being really hurt by another person and being unable to figure out a way to defend myself. My bad perm is a story of disappointment and wounding. We all have a bad perm story. We all have letdowns and hurts of varying degrees that become parts of the stories we write about life. Those stories determine our attitudes, and those attitudes will always lead to action.

When David came upon Nabal and Abigail that day, three stories were being written, and three attitudes were revealed. Nabal authored a story of self-centeredness and greed. David authored a story of insecurity and impulsiveness. And Abigail authored a story of trust and courage. I have to believe that Nabal, David, and Abigail all had been wounded before, but the way they integrated that story into an attitude was very different.

Understanding the attitude we bring to our stories is like finding the compass of our souls. The attitude is the arrow of the compass, and our thoughts, words, and actions will always follow the setting of that attitude.

Truth #2: Our characters are formed one moment at a time.

First Samuel 25 shows us one fateful day in the lives of Nabal, David, and Abigail. But the choices made that day were not spontaneous. They were a soul-jerk reaction to the attitude each had already established. That attitude was formed by the character of each, which was developed one moment at a time. George Dana Boardman, a missionary serving in Burma, once said, "Let us not say, Every man is the architect of his own fortune; but let us say, Every man is the architect of his own character." We don't have control over the wounding experiences in our lives. But we do have a responsibility for the way we integrate those experiences into the story.

Nabal's, David's, and Abigail's characters weren't formed during this conflict. When the pressure was on, their characters were displayed. Nabal's rigid, bitter spirit was exposed. David's impetuous but repentant spirit came through. Abigail's deliberate and wise spirit was revealed.

Character is not formed instantaneously in moments of pressure; rather, it's in moments of pressure that we discover what's already been formed in our souls.

The big moments of our lives don't shape our characters either—those big moments just reveal the character that's already in place. It's in the quiet, unseen moments that our characters are formed. It's in the daily choices we make that the compass of our attitudes is set and reset. It's a long, slow series of choices that build the foundation of our souls. Character is not formed instantaneously in moments of pressure; rather, it's in moments of pressure that we discover what's already been formed in our souls.

Truth #3: Being wise in earthly matters starts by understanding the business of heaven.

Abigail is the only character in this story who, from beginning to end, operated under the main tenet of wisdom: *God is greatest, and He knows best.* When faced with a high-pressure situation, Abigail wasted no time acting from what she believed. She not only lived out that story, she called David to author a better story about his own life. In her passionate dialogue with David, she revealed the substance of her character. During their dialogue, she

- called on God's sovereignty (verses 26 and 30)
- admonished David to be his best (verse 28)
- told David what God could do (verse 28)
- reminded David of what God had already done (verse 29)
- spoke in faith about what God would do (verses 28 and 30)

Although this story makes me want to be more like Abigail, we can learn from all three of the main players. We are all like Nabal sometimes. Parts of our stories feel rigid and petrified, as if they could never be integrated into the whole of us. We react from anger or pride. All of us are like David sometimes. Parts of our lives feel as if they were born out of insecurity and wounding. We feel as if we've been waiting too long for God to work, so we want to act impulsively to feel better today instead of waiting with faith for tomorrow. And all of us have the opportunity to be like Abigail. Like her, we can reset our attitude on the business of heaven, where we stake our lives on the truth that *God is greatest, and He knows best.* Second Timothy 1:7 says, "The Spirit God gave us does not make us timid, but gives us power, love and self-discipline." Abigail is this verse in living color.

Remember: **Who We Are + Moments That Matter = Stories We Live.** How is your story of yesterday shaping the story of tomorrow?

Keeping It Real

Do you have a "perm story" in your past? If so, how did that event shape your attitude? If not, what moments have determined the way you think or feel toward life? Toward God? Toward other people? Toward yourself?

Place your attitude ("settled way of thinking or feeling") on the continuum below:

Bitter ———————————————— Yielded
to God

Writing your ———————————— Believing in
own story   God's story

Anxious in ———————————— Trusting God in
my situation   my situation

4

The Voices

The Party in Your Head

> The greatest enemy of any one of our
> truths may be the rest of our truths.
>
> WILLIAM JAMES

I learned a helpful counselor's adage early in my therapy days: Whatever brings a person into the counseling office is usually not the real problem. Think of the couple who divorce because the husband hangs the toilet paper the wrong way. (Who knew the bathroom would be the make-or-break room of the house for marriages?) Of course, it's not about the toilet paper. It's about what the toilet paper represents in that marriage, like the inability to listen to each other, to yield to each other, or to openly communicate and respond to each other's needs. It's about two people whose own stories of hurt and sin collide, and they can't find their way out of the rubble.

The memories that shape our narratives are not really about the actual relationships or events. Our stories are created around the interpretation of those events, as well as the shape, color, and feel those memories create in our past. When we author our own stories, there is no such thing as a pure analysis. When viewed through our own lenses, the truth is polluted indeed.

My home perm of '89, then, was not really about the perm. For all of us, it's never really about the perm, the award, the breakup, or scoring the winning goal in the final soccer game of your high school career. (I've never scored a winning goal; I just threw that in for you athletes.) It's always about much more than the memory itself. It's the interpretation of that memory that shapes our understanding of ourselves as actors on this great stage of life, our success as agents of our destinies, and the account we write as the authors of our own stories.

But here's where it gets really important: *The way we remember yesterday profoundly shapes the choices we make today.* We are not impartial decision makers, interpreting each new moment of choice from a position of neutrality. We are not like Switzerland. In fact, the way our memories drive us is more like a frenzied South American dictator.

The way we remember yesterday profoundly shapes the choices we make today.

Our memories are dramatic and often lead us to make sweeping generalizations about our past, present, and future.

Even the memories we try to forget have a loud and

demanding voice at the party that is our brains. Psychologists who study repressed memories find that the brain has a special system to deal with painful and negative memories (that's the good ol' extrasynaptic GABA receptors, for all you nerds out there). Recent studies show that we are more likely to remember those painful events when our mood is similar to how we felt in the original event.[1] So why does it matter that you know about extrasynaptic GABA receptors, other than sounding smart at your next cocktail party? Although the studies done specifically target high-trauma memories, I believe the same concept holds true for the memories of our past struggles. When we get stressed, when we deal with a situation that makes us feel exposed, angry, or ashamed, we tend to jump back to those same memories in our past, looking for a story line to follow. The party in our minds looks to that memory to tell us what to expect. And even if we thought we'd locked that memory in a closet, it finds a way to make itself known. Left unchecked, we will let the interpretation of our past experiences direct our responses to future events.

Allow me to once again talk about the perm situation, or what we shall now call the Perm Incident of '89. When I emerged from that half-bath/torture chamber of a "salon" with hair so frizzy and fried that I could have signed up to be a Ronald McDonald mascot, I wasn't just dealing with loss of hope that my hair would catapult me into the preteen cool set. The perm became a symbol of much more. The damaged hair and damaged emotions marked a moment in time when I authored a story about myself and other people, and subsequently, God. The story line was something like this:

If you don't look right, people will notice and make fun of you. No one will like you if you stick out. If you stand up for yourself, you'll get beaten down, so it's better to blend in. People are mean, and if you make any mistakes, you will pay for them. The only way to survive is to always get everything just right and not let anyone get too close.

Of course, if the Perm Incident of '89 had been an isolated struggle, the voice might not have been quite so demanding at the party in my head. But when one painful struggle reminds you of another, that isolated voice has a friend. And when one more struggle reinforces that voice, you have a trio, and before long, it's a screamo[2] band of shame, just waiting to shout out the "truth" with every subsequent struggle that plucks the right chord. *It's never about the perm.*

We all have a tendency to interpret our struggles and let them define our future stories. Author John Eldredge writes about this in his book *Waking the Dead.* The way we interpret our struggles, he says, becomes our truth, or what I refer to as our capital-*s* Struggle. Eldredge says this darkness has worked in human hearts since the Fall; it's a force that wants to veil us from the true glory that is ours in Christ. This glory is the "truest part of us,"[3] and to live in that glory is to be fully ourselves, the way God intended. The agreements we make with ourselves about our struggles are the stories that cover up this true self. If this true self is better than any covered-up version, why wouldn't I just want to be her, despite bad perms and hard rejections? As the apostle Paul so aptly said in Romans 7, why would I want one thing but do another? Truly, why is the struggle so real?

I'd like to ask you to consider something that might go against your common sensibilities. But hang with me: What if the struggle isn't just about the things you've done wrong and the things that have been done wrong to you? What if you've believed an ultimate lie about yourself, that something in your truest self is actually wrong and unworthy? The Bible tells us that this struggle isn't being waged only within yourself, but is happening in the heavenly realms. Scripture clearly shows that humanity has an enemy. This part of you—the true, unashamed, fully glorious self, fully living in the image of God who made her—she has an enemy.

In the Bible, evil is personified in a presence that enters into conversation with humans. In Genesis 3:1, we see evil personified in the serpent, who challenged Eve with the question "Did God really say . . . ?" He uses this conversation to lure Eve into a dialogue in which he calls into question God's intentions. In Matthew 4:3, we hear this same voice again testing Jesus: "If you are the Son of God . . ." The enemy uses this opening line to try to ensnare Jesus in a conversation that calls into doubt His identity. Paul talks about the results of this darkness in Titus 3:3: "At one time we too were foolish, disobedient, *deceived* and enslaved by all kinds of passions and pleasures. We lived in malice and envy, being hated and hating one another" (emphasis added).

Our enemy uses the same tactics with us. Once he gets us to doubt God and to doubt ourselves, he capitalizes on that deception to turn us against each other. Words like *foolish*, *disobedient, deceived,* and *enslaved* become the plot in our stories, even when we don't recognize it. But the fruit of this dark wisdom results in fractures of all kinds—doubt in God's existence and goodness; deep wounds in our grasp of our identity, the very core of who we are; guarded, angry, and wounded hearts that lash out at others, fracturing the gift of intimacy and community with those we love.

Paul calls out the enemy as one who "masquerades as an angel of light" (2 Corinthians 11:14). The enemy uses lures that seem truthful and then twists them to his purposes to deceive us. Peter calls the enemy a roaring lion on the prowl, looking to devour (1 Peter 5:8). The enemy uses intentional, violent tactics that lead to destruction. In the Perm Incident, he used a normal coming-of-age experience as a weapon. As a result, I didn't see my bad hair days (okay, months) as an opportunity to grow through an imperfect struggle, but as proof that my imperfection was a liability that I would always have to strive to overcome. A not-good-enough perm made me think of myself as a not-good-enough person.

Whatever moments in our lives have left an imprint on our souls—whether places of struggle and strife or even places of victory and pride—all are opportunities for the darkness to try to take the pen out of our hands and write the story for us. The enemy is at work wherever he sees an opportunity to get us to believe a story that calls into doubt God's true intentions for us. Whatever moments we remember in our souls that work as bludgeons to crack us open, to fracture our love for ourselves and for others, come from the work of the enemy and the power of sin.

Wisdom at Work

Maybe that's why, when James contrasts the difference between wisdom from heaven and wisdom "from below," he uses such harsh and dark language:

> Who is wise and understanding among you? Let them show it by their good life, by deeds done in the humility that comes from wisdom. But if you harbor bitter envy and selfish ambition in your hearts, do not boast about it or deny the truth. Such "wisdom" does not come down from heaven but is earthly, unspiritual, demonic. For where you have envy and selfish ambition, there you find disorder and every evil practice.
>
> JAMES 3:13-16

We know that darkness has been at work in the disordered places in our hearts. A disordered life lacks cohesion and clarity. Instead of wholeness, there is fracture. Instead of peace, there is anxiety. Instead of trust, there is doubt. And instead of truth, there is deceit. Every part of our struggle that stays disordered has been smeared dirty with darkness and the power of sin and death.

And we thought we were just talking about perms! But friend—*it's never about the perm. It's always about what those memories do to our stories—our interpretation of both God and ourselves in light of our struggles.*

When we began this journey together, I mentioned that you might not want to read this book if you were looking for comfy-cozy Christianity. But there is hope if you are tired of the disordered soul. You may know that you have your own perm story (or another story of wounding, fear, or shame). You may recognize the moments that led to seasons of deceit, darkness, bitterness, strife, and other kinds of unspiritual "wisdom." If so, then it's time to demand the pen back from your enemy so you can author a better story, one that integrates the struggle and the hardship into an understanding of what happened when darkness entered in and how you can find your way back into the light. In order to reclaim that story, you need to understand the story that we all share, the one revealed to us in God's Word.

Summarizing the Original Plot

So where do these disordered and disruptive voices originate? In *Jesus: A Theography*, theologians Leonard Sweet and Frank Viola summarize the dark plot of the human story as a broken relationship in four parts:

A broken relationship with God. Sin entered humanity's story through the generations before us, stemming back to that first deception in the Garden. Sin enters our personal stories when we agree with the darkness about how we interpret our own stories, turning away from God and doubting His goodness.

A broken relationship with ourselves. "We're all wearing masks, facades, and trying to be something other than what God made us,"[4] say Sweet and Viola. Sin enters with the inevitable companion, shame. Shame causes us to hide and disguise our true and vulnerable soul, first and foremost, from our own conscious "self." We actually hide our true soul from our own self in an attempt to be something we are not. This is the second twist of deception, turning our original brokenness with God into brokenness with ourselves.

A broken relationship with each other. The third maniacal twist of deception comes when we begin to regard one another as competitors and enemies. The wounds that have never been healed in our own lives become the weapons we use against each other. We believe the point of our stories is to claw our way into our self-created peace and happiness, and others become either stepping-stones or obstacles along the way. We use words and wounds as weapons against one another, hurting and being hurt in this endless quest to use one another to find fulfillment.

A broken relationship with the world. Our unredeemed past clouds our judgment for the future, and as the stories we author settle into our souls, we view the rest of the world through them. Our wounds become everyone's wounds. Our struggles become our own gospel truth, and with a final twist of his sword, the enemy of our souls places the deepest cut right where he began—into the intentions and power of God. When this happens, our own struggles become the lens through which we view the world, and the gospel of Jesus Christ loses all power in our lives. War, violence, and the careless and heavy-handed way we treat the environment all become by-products of our deep wounds. We believe the most damaging lie of all:

God has been distant from me, so God is distant from everything.

God is not at work in my heart, so God is not at work in the world.

I am on my own.

I have been abandoned.

You see, it's definitely not about the perm. It's not about your parents' divorce. It's not about your depression. It's not about the insecurities that hang around your neck like an industrial-strength chain, dragging your head down into the dirt. It's not about the trinkets of accomplishment you collect to feel good about yourself. It's about the original story of sin, written long before you were born and calling itself the only true reality, not only for you but for your children. It's the four-way brokenness that threatens to define your life and the lives you influence.

If you've carried around a secret burden, feeling like your struggles affect you much more deeply than you want to admit, perhaps it's because this burden of sin and shame is far heavier than you can carry. Maybe your struggles feel dramatic because they *are* dramatic—a shattering of your true design, your free soul, your joyful purpose. Whether it's a middle school rejection or a grown-up infidelity, your struggles point to the bigger, broken story of humanity, the story in which we are all unwitting actors.

A New Story

We don't have to look any further than our newsfeeds to know that life is deeply broken. We don't need more than an honest second with our own hearts to know that a force lurks in our own shadows, constantly writing our stories out of the stories of our past, reinforcing our deepest fears and claiming that nothing will really change. We fear that we must remain vigilant to those around us or they will hurt us and that we are essentially not worth it.

The "it" in your "not worth it" is the variation that is unique to you. Maybe it's that deep lie you believe that you aren't worth that person's time. That you aren't worth loving. That you aren't worth protecting. That you aren't valuable. That you aren't enjoyable.

Sound familiar? The enemy may be powerful, but he's not that creative. He uses whatever "it" is for you to enforce and reinforce the same message, the same broken-record message of wounds, shame, guilt, and sin. Yes, I'm talking to you, Christian-since-birth. Yes, you, Sunday school story champion. Maybe it's the ones who've been closest to the true story who are the most likely to take it for granted.

One of the most honest and heart-wrenching questions people ask me is "How do I know God loves me?" A reader named Brent recently sent this to me:

> I can't say Romans 8:16 has ever happened to me.
> I've never felt the Holy Spirit testify to my spirit
> that I am his child.
>
> Maybe I'm not? Maybe I've deluded myself?
>
> How do I know I love God? I mean, I know I want
> to obey and that's what Jesus says we'll do if we love
> him. I just don't have that love feeling like you know
> you feel over your own child or husband or mom.

This is a churchgoing "good" guy. This is you and me. This is all of us, in some form or another. You may not doubt God's love, but maybe you doubt His power. You may not doubt His power, but maybe you've given up on your healing. You may not think you need healing, but maybe you can acknowledge a current of cynicism within you as you have given up on wonder, adventure, and the great mystery of God at work in your soul and in the world.

Good Desperation

I like to think of this part of the story as the good desperate part. I liken it to my labor with our third child. The first few hours went well, but the last ones were almost unbearable. I have one vague memory of yelling out for Jesus. Don't get me wrong, I love Jesus, but it's out of character for me to be so vocal and violent in crying for Him. A few minutes later, Desmond Peter was born.

Maybe the places in our stories that feel the most broken and unusable are actually the ones that give us the energy to seek Him in all honesty and desperation.

My midwife told me later, "It always works when they cry out to Jesus." Of course, it was funny trying to imagine Jesus as the midwife of every desperate woman in labor. I picture Him just waiting for them to call on His name so He can send the baby into the world. But maybe there's some truth in it.

Maybe we are all struggling in labor to get back to the true story. Maybe we all need to get to that frenzied place where we don't care anymore what anyone really thinks—we just know we need to cry out to Jesus. Maybe the places in our stories that feel the most broken and unusable are actually the ones that give us the energy to seek Him in all honesty and desperation.

The good desperation is where we can pray these verses with full honesty:

Evening, morning and noon
   I cry out in distress,
   and he hears my voice.
PSALM 55:17

LORD, you are the God who saves me;
   day and night I cry out to you.
PSALM 88:1

If you call out for insight
   and cry aloud for understanding, . . .
then you will understand the fear of the LORD
   and find the knowledge of God.
PROVERBS 2:3, 5

When we are desperate in this good way, we seek God with a different kind of intensity and consistency. It's an around-the-clock looking for Him. It's seeking Him with all of our hearts and minds, just as we search when we have lost something really valuable. Think of the anxiety we feel when we lose our phone or keys or wallet. When we've lost something important, we think about it all the time. Every room we enter, we find ourselves looking for it, and in our quest we return to the same places over and over. We ask others to help us find our prized possession. We think about it when we wake up and when we go to sleep. (Can you tell I've lost a lot of valuable things in my life?) If only we looked for God's direction in the same way!

Good desperation leads us to give up on our own version of the story and ask God to be the author of the story.

Second Samuel 22:25 says, "GOD rewrote the text of my life when I opened the book of my heart to his eyes" (MSG). Good desperation is the opening of the book of our hearts to God and telling Him: *Okay, God, I lay it before You. I've been living from the broken story, and I am desperate for something different. As I open it all to You, I will trust that you are greatest, and You know best. Tell me the story of my heart, the true and uncut version.*

The wisdom from heaven is pure. It leads to the unadulterated, unashamed cry of our hearts to Jesus, asking Him to teach us how to reinterpret the equation that makes up our stories:

Who We Are + Moments That Matter = Stories We Live

Those of us who want clean and quick answers will be frustrated by this process. In order to look ahead, we must look back. In order to trust God's wisdom, we have to know God's heart. In order to write a new story, we have to be willing to rewrite the old story. In order to interpret our today struggles, we have to understand the big Struggle that got us here in the first place. This is the way forward, but it takes the good kind of desperation, the moment when we give up on telling the story, when we stop listening to the party in our heads and turn our ears to the one Voice of Truth.

The Unveiled Story

There's a crazy and incredible story in the Gospels about the time when Jesus' glory was revealed. It lasted only a moment, and only His three closest friends were there to see it. Jesus had led them up to a high mountain, where He was "transfigured"—which literally means "to give a new and typically exalted . . . appearance to."[5] The apostle Matthew writes that Jesus' "face shone like the sun, and his clothes became as white as the light" (17:2).

In that instant, Jesus' friends saw the true story—their leader, in glorious light, conversing with Elijah and Moses, the great prophets of the Old Testament. As hard as it might be, just try to imagine seeing Jesus—the guy you eat meals with, walk with, and do life with—imagine seeing Him for who He really is in this otherworldly, mysterious experience.

Then as Jesus talked with Moses and Elijah, a voice from heaven said, "This is my Son, whom I love; with him I am well pleased. Listen to him!" (verse 5). I don't know why the disciples weren't terrified until then, but this voice sent them over the edge. They fell to the ground. Maybe it was the voice thundering in their souls that helped them see what was really happening before them, the fact that a whole other story was going on, one they didn't realize or couldn't see until that moment. Everything the disciples had believed about Moses and Elijah, the great captains of their Jewish faith, was being rewritten in this moment. All they had thought to be true about God and His ways was being transfigured alongside Jesus. Jesus was the true story. Knowing Him meant that everything they understood before was reinterpreted in the light of His presence, and everything they anticipated for the future was rewritten because of His love.

The command of God to Jesus' disciples—*Listen to Him*—is still the command today. When we listen to our Lord, we allow God to rewrite our stories with Jesus as the main character. The new equation looks something like this:

$$\frac{(\text{Who We Are} + \text{Moments That Matter})}{\text{Jesus in the Moments}} = \text{Transfigured Story}$$

Sorry for the algebra equation, but it's the best representation I can create! Good desperation leads us back into our stories, into the moments that have told us what role we play in the world (actor), what power we have over the world (agent), and what story is true for us (author). Our new story becomes a transfigured story when Christ transforms it. We'll get to how that works in the second half of this book.

When Brent asked me about knowing God's love, I could point him to Bible verses and encourage him to accept God's Word as true for him. However, the struggle wasn't with Brent's knowledge; it was with his heart. How do we understand God's love? How do we know about our purpose?

Every question and every desperate place of hurt and longing invites us to solve this equation from God's perspective. The struggle is real, but when we invite Jesus into our moments, the struggle is also good.

It is in the honest reflection of our struggles that we will finally ask the most important question of our lives: "Where is Jesus in my story?"

Keeping It Real

1. Do you resonate with the "party in my head" analogy? What voices are you most prone to hear and listen to in your story (some possibilities: shame, independence, anger, pride, love, fear, hope, trust, etc.)?

2. Our original story details brokenness in four parts: with God, with ourselves, with others, and with the world. Which of those elements most resonates with you? How have you experienced the effects in your life?

3. Good desperation leads us to seek God. Can you think of a moment that might have seemed insignificant at the time, but actually was a place of good desperation? What questions do you find yourself asking in times of good desperation?

5

The Vision
The Real Story

Jesus, as Lord of time, is able to do what
we cannot: He can heal those wounds of
the past that still cause us suffering.

FRANCIS MACNUTT

In my early years as a counselor, people occasionally asked
me what kind of therapy I practiced, which always made
me feel squirmy and uncertain. Counselors can practice
cognitive-behavioral, solution-focused, or dialectical behavior therapy—or other treatments with labels designed to
make them sound complicated and expensive. My counseling practice didn't adhere strictly to any of those designa-
tions, which is why I probably belonged in ministry and
not in counseling. At one point I learned that when counselors say they have an "eclectic" practice, it means they mix
everything together and use what works best. I, too, took an
eclectic approach to my counseling, which basically meant

I hung on for dear life as people told me their stories. I also experienced the good desperation of needing Jesus in each and every one of those relationships.

When it came to being a Christian and being a counselor, I found myself in a constant tension: *Who is healing this person—is it due to something they find within themselves or through a relationship with Jesus? Is Jesus in people's stories even when they don't acknowledge Him as a presence? Do we create truth, or is there an objective, uncut version of truth out there somewhere, something we can access?* For my achievement-loving, insecure self, I often wondered what success looked like in counseling. Counselors like to tell clients that success is when the client doesn't need the counselor anymore, but when people stop making appointments, it either means you were really good or really terrible at your job, so that metric kind of evens out, doesn't it?

Because those questions don't have simple answers, most of what I learned in counseling was how to listen really closely. I was trying to identify the story themes that emerged over the course of time, from early memories of joy and pain into a patient's present season of dryness, stuckness, or sadness. I read psychological theories and found aspects in each that aligned with my understanding of God and people—the "unconditional positive regard" described by Carl Rogers, the hidden power of our "shadow" from Carl Jung, the theory on self and our inability to overcome our instinctual drives posited by Sigmund Freud. I loved that William Glasser coined the term *reality therapy* and had great success with clients by helping them deal with their real needs and the reality of their choices.

But all of it fell somewhat short in the counseling office. My office door became a threshold between two stories. Outside the door, all my clients looked like normal people who were handling life pretty well. They took showers, wore matching clothes, held jobs, and had some friends. But when they crossed my threshold, the self-created images of an okay life fell away, and they poured out their stories of loss, hurt, confusion, and struggle. Every psychological theory was helpful, but it was never enough. Each one fell short when it came to understanding and interpreting the stories of the hurt, disenfranchised, and beaten-down souls who came to my office. My greatest lesson from the thousands of stories I heard in that office was my own form of reality therapy: Without Christ, there is no real freedom.

My profound theory of self applies not only to people who know they are far from God but also to those who were raised in the church. Because *without Christ, there is no real freedom* is true of everyone who has not applied the power of Christ to their story, who has not allowed Jesus, who stands outside of time, to permeate the past, present, and future of their story. We can have all the information about Jesus' power without it actually affecting our lives. We can sing about the power of Christ's resurrection without experiencing His resurrecting power in our stories. If we experience Christ only partway or only on Sundays, we cannot expect a change. Our stories require a full overhaul.

This is why the concept of God's wisdom is so fascinating. When James talks about the wisdom from heaven, he is talking about the wisdom of Christ that transforms our understanding of our stories. He tells us, "The wisdom from above is . . . open to reason" (James 3:17, ESV). God takes the weak, the shameful, and the foolish things in life to lead us to the ultimate source of wisdom, found in Jesus Christ. First Corinthians 1:26-30 explains that the very places of struggle become the places of victory in Christ, who becomes the main character in our stories, "who has become for us wisdom from God" (verse 30). It is in Christ that we discover that "everything that we have—right thinking and right living, a clean slate and a fresh start—comes from God by way of Jesus Christ" (verse 30, MSG).

William Glasser's reality therapy attempts to deal only with the present, avoiding the past. But God's form of reality therapy invites us to deal with the whole, honest truth of ourselves, both past and present, and to invite Christ to transfigure our entire story with His redeeming grace. Jesus is a time traveler in our stories, moving freely from early chapters of identity, showing up in unexpected places in our present, sealing promises in the future. As we get to know Jesus, as we interact with Him through the stories of the Bible, we will discover the way He gently treats all our struggles, from regret to sin to forgiveness to healing. We will see that He is not just the author of our faith, but the author of the whole story, the invisible presence at every turn.

Because God is not bound by time, He can reach back into our stories in a way that rewrites our memories and our interpretation of ourselves. Here's an example: One of my friends had a painfully abusive relationship with her father growing up. She stuffed the memories for a long time, but when she struggled to be close to her husband, she sought help to understand her difficulty.

Jesus traveling through her story required her to revisit her painful memories and invite Him into them. Only then could she recognize the lies these memories had convinced her to believe: that she was unworthy, that she brought the mistreatment on herself, that it was dangerous to open herself up to anyone. Once that deception had been exposed, my friend was able to accept as truth that her heavenly Father loved her and saw her as His precious child. Over time, the transformed story led to some different interpretations of her experience. Although terribly painful, the new story led to compassion toward her father, recognizing the brokenness that led him to abuse her in the first place. She also slowly began to forgive her dad—which she directly attributes to experiencing God's love for her in her life. The memories that held her captive for decades no longer had power over her. Rewriting her story of pain and shame in the past also freed her to move closer to her husband in the present. That kind of miracle is what Jesus can do.

The New Story

One of the most powerful experiences I've had in ministry is the reality therapy of encouraging people to deal honestly with their lives. This often happens as they tell their uncut stories—not the ones that read like résumés, but the real ones . . . the ones that reveal the four-way broken places in their lives. I've heard church leaders speak poignantly of fractures between family members, painful woundings in their childhoods, seasons of great loss. I've heard twenty-somethings speak of their drug use, their rebellion, and the painful loss of idealism that comes from being the child of a divorce or of an alcoholic. I know these examples sound overly dramatic, but this is real life for real people you might think have it all together. Real life is great men and women of God who've been lost. Real life is earnest and fun young adults who've been crushed. And the realest kinds of life are their stories of rescue, redemption, and transformation in Christ.

When we talk about going back in order to move forward, our hearts recognize the brokenness in our past that is keeping us stuck. The Spirit of God has an extraordinary ability to move gently through our hearts, to trace over scars and alert us to those wounds that aren't truly healed, the ones that are tender and perhaps even still open, stitched together roughly with our own clumsy attempts to move on. Yet I also know that God uses our brokenness to lead us to good desperation. He brings us to the end of the road so we will stop running at breakneck speed on our own self-created path. Knowing Christ's strength in the weak places is what gives us the ability to stop trying to sprint past our past and instead to obey Him in our present and trust Him with our future.

Knowing Christ's strength in the weak places is what gives us the ability to obey Him in our present and trust Him with our future.

How can we interpret our stories in light of God's goodness and grace? Psalm 107 gives us a place to start. It begins, "Give thanks to the LORD, for he is good; his love endures forever." That's not so different from our pledge of wisdom: *God is greatest, and He knows best.* The psalm goes on to describe how God rescues us at just the right time in our lives, reversing the brokenness and bringing us satisfaction and wholeness. There are four story themes that tell of how people come to know the presence and goodness of God in their lives. You might find you resonate deeply with one of these four or with different aspects of each one. Let's take a look at those themes and see where you might find God in your story.

Story Theme #1: Lost

The first vignette in Psalm 107 tells of those who "wandered in desert wastelands, finding no way to a city where they could settle" (verse 4). To be lost is to be disoriented and unsure of the right way to go. We may still be living and active, but we find ourselves hopelessly adrift.

I have a friend in her sixties who recently came to faith. She's a dignified, well-educated woman who always seems to have the right word for everything. When she describes her experience of faith, she speaks in a reverent way that makes people listen. She recently came to my office to talk about being baptized. She arranged herself in a chair, her legs swept to the side and crossed at the ankles. She held her purse on her lap and told me her story. She talked of divorce, a difficult diagnosis, and a deep place in her soul that was seeking more. This beautiful, wise woman said to me simply, "I was lost, really." The difference between how this woman appeared and what she said about herself was jarring. *Lost.*

Something about the word *lost* brings out the child in us. To be lost is to have exhausted all possibilities of finding our own way. To be lost is to be helpless. To be truly lost is to acknowledge that we do not have it in ourselves to find the path. Psalm 107 says some of us will wander, unable to find our way. We may seek to settle, to be settled, but we cannot find that place of rest. But God promises to deliver those who cry out to Him in their trouble. He will lead them on a straight way and satisfy their hunger and thirst (verses 7 and 9).

In chapter 15 of the Gospel of Luke, Jesus picks up on this theme in the parables of the lost sheep, the lost coin, and finally the lost son, one of the most well-known stories in Scripture. The prodigal son willfully wanders (taking his inheritance and leaving). Eventually, when all seems lost, the son regains clarity (he comes to his senses about his lostness). The turning point of the story is this moment of lucidity, when the son realizes all that he has lost. He has wandered so far from the goodness of his father that he considers himself unworthy to even claim that relationship anymore, saying, "I am no longer worthy to be called your son" (verse 21). But in an expression of the true nature of our Father in heaven, the father in this story, who has been waiting for his son's return, runs to embrace the prodigal, declaring that "he was lost and is found" (verse 24). The promise of Psalm 107:9, "he satisfies the thirsty and fills the hungry with good things," is illustrated in the lost son, whose reversal of fortune comes even though he was the one who wandered away.

Is coming home your story?

Story Theme #2: Bound

Psalm 107:10 describes a different form of adversity: "Some sat in darkness and deepest gloom, imprisoned in iron chains of misery" (NLT). In this next vignette, people found themselves prisoners, bound in their own rebellion. By deliberately choosing to disregard the words of God and reject His way, they had become slaves. Interestingly, the psalm does not specify to what country or leader these prisoners became slaves. Perhaps the psalmist was deliberately ambiguous to allow readers to interpret for themselves exactly what their bondage looks like.

Once we begin to live by any other law but God's law, the chains lock on. It takes only one act to bind us in those chains. Every time we think in our hearts, *I will do it my way*, every time we disregard God's command to worship Him alone, every time we give our hearts, minds, or bodies to some "other" in the hopes that it will give us the fulfillment and freedom we seek, we've rebelled and become enslaved.

This is an unpopular line of thinking in our day, when we attribute the wrong we do to the wrong done to us. In other words, we assume that because we've been hurt along the way, we now have the right to live as we choose and to hurt others. Our world promotes this scapegoat mentality, encouraging us to claim our own good intentions even as we continue to break the four-way relationships with God, ourselves, others, and the world.

But there is a "reap what you sow" truth at work here. If we sow bitterness and wounding, we should expect to bitterly wound others. If we sow fear, we will be subject to fear. In a true show of "sow and reap" mentality, those who rebel against God's counsel will find themselves enslaved "because they rebelled against God's commands and despised the plans of the Most High" (Psalm 107:11). This is not a punishment for the sake of punishment; it's a law of nature—we will reap what we sow. Romans 6:16 says, "You are slaves of the one you obey."

I recently read an article written by a father of adult daughters about the false promises of "a sexual revolution that has lost sight of any boundaries." The author beseeched other dads "to love enough to speak unpopular truths when the world cheats your children with fifty shades of grey." After all, "if all women are yearning for is strings-free sex, why does it seem to require so much alcohol?"[1] Clearly, his words hit home, as the article garnered more than eight hundred comments. As the writer pointed out, though the world claims sexual empowerment leads to freedom, sexual behavior outside of God's design is ironically—and even diabolically—enslaving. The greatest trick the enemy can pull on humanity is to convince us that enslaving behaviors will bring freedom and to depict God's path to true freedom as bondage. And since the first whisper in the Garden, that's been the party line of darkness.

We find this upside-down mentality of what brings freedom and enslavement in the story of God's chosen people, the Hebrews. After centuries of enslavement by the Egyptians, they were set free *to* life in God, but they jeopardized that life by creating their own rules about what "free" meant. And then just three generations after God led them into the Promised Land, His people had turned completely away from His stipulations for freedom. In a haunting declaration of what happens when people disregard God, the book of Judges reports that "another generation grew up who knew neither the LORD nor what he had done for Israel. . . . They followed and worshiped various gods of the peoples around them. . . . They were in great distress" (Judges 2:10, 12, 15).

If we look closely throughout history, we find that freedom is always superficial and shoddy when it means "do whatever we want." We buy the lie that freedom means acting without authority or restraint, but then find that exact belief leads us to a deceptive self-bondage where we become slaves to our needy inner gremlin, always grasping for more but never satisfied. We discover that we need someone to set us free because we do not have the power to become free ourselves. Freedom is always in the hands of the One who gives it.

Once again, the poetic expression of bondage and freedom in Psalm 107 comes to life in the words and actions of Jesus. In Mark 5, Jesus took a trip across the Sea of Galilee and "a man with an impure spirit came from the tombs to meet him" (verse 2). The passage tells us that nothing—neither people (he lived alone in the tombs) nor chains (he broke the irons on his feet)—could bind the man. "No one was strong enough to subdue him" (verse 4). Haunted by powerful spirits, he wandered day and night in this desolate place, crying out and cutting himself with stones. In this star-tling and heart-wrenching picture of oppression, we see dark-ness at work, which ultimately turns humanity against itself. This man wandered among the dead, and in some ways, was worse off than the dead themselves.

Sometimes I wonder what it would be like if we could see souls the way God sees them. I wonder how many men and women are like this, wandering around with empty eyes and vacant faces. Their degradation and misery cannot be healed by any human efforts. Sometimes I wonder if our obsession with being able to explain every condition and malady of the spirit has kept us from acknowledging that there is mystery. There is spirit. There is darkness.

Despite the pit-in-your-stomach picture of this man's life, there is a force more powerful than this darkness. That force is hope. "When he saw Jesus from a distance, he ran and fell on his knees in front of him. He shouted at the top of his voice, 'What do you want with me, Jesus, Son of the Most High God?'" (Mark 5:6-7). Oh, yes, "even the demons believe [in God] and shudder" (James 2:19).

When Jesus entered this man's life, He set him free from the powerful forces that had attacked his dignity and human-ity. When the townspeople nearby heard what had happened, they came to see Jesus and saw the man, "sitting there, dressed and in his right mind" (Mark 5:15). When Jesus prepared to leave, the man begged to go with Him. But Jesus wanted him to stay in the place of his previous bondage. He wanted the man to return to his family and "tell them how much the Lord has done for you, and how he has had mercy on you" (verse 19). You see, when Christ sets us free *from* something or someone, He sets us free *to* something or someone. We become God's chosen instrument to declare that freedom in the place of our wounding to the people who have known us in our bondage. We are set free to a responsibility to declare that freedom.

> Let them give thanks to the LORD for his unfailing love
> and his wonderful deeds for mankind,
> for he breaks down gates of bronze
> and cuts through bars of iron.
>
> PSALM 107:15-16

Is deliverance your story?

Story Theme #3: Afflicted

Psalm 107:17 describes how we become foolish: "Some became fools through their rebellious ways and suffered affliction because of their iniquities."

There are all kinds of foolishness in this world, but not a single living one of us wants to admit that we can fall into this kind of living. It may be okay to be unintentionally foolish—like the time I went to the airport without my license. I was let through security using my Costco membership card, but I still had to rent a car when I arrived. Oops. Or the time I scheduled a retreat too close to an international trip. I had to have my best friend pick me up at the airport and drive my jet-lag-dragging self six hours into the boonies to teach in an international daze. Double oops. (Thank you, Jesus, for grace.)

But almost no one wants to admit that we can cross over from unintentional foolishness ("oopsie") to "I'm doing it again" (on purpose—with a nod to vintage Britney Spears). Foolish actions lead to foolish attitudes, which become a persistent pattern of living. This is how we go from foolish actions to "becoming fools," as detailed in the third vignette in Psalm 107.

Rebellious ways lead to foolish patterns that bring on affliction. The reap-and-sow mentality continues, and in this section, we read of the wounding that results from foolish living. The psalmist does not talk of what led to the foolish behavior in the first place—there is just the straight-truth mentality that foolish actions led to suffering. We may have made those mistakes because of our bad upbringing or past history, but we still have to live with the reality of our mistakes.

I recently hurt a friend of mine with my careless actions. Of course, I didn't do it on purpose, but over the course of several weeks, I did not prioritize our friendship. By putting other things first, I hurt her feelings not once, not twice, but on four different occasions. I was so oblivious that I didn't realize it had happened until she stopped answering my calls. I drove over to her house one morning and knocked on her door. The results of my actions had caught up with me; I had undervalued my friend by putting other pressing needs first. I explained myself to her, but my friend was under no obligation to believe me or forgive me, because I was clearly in the wrong. Thankfully, she quickly forgave me. But foolish actions always have ramifications. It doesn't matter if my reasons were valid or not—there are still consequences.

In the psalm, the consequences of persistent foolish behavior led to a pervasive illness of the soul with spiritual, physical, and emotional ramifications. The psalmist's use of the word *affliction* is a poetic way of saying that hard living leads to painful lives. Such lives are full of unhealthy habits, broken relationships, and repeated patterns of negative thinking and living. Recent research corroborates the theory that perpetual cynicism, hostility, and anger are all linked to higher mortality rates.[2] Truly, as the psalmist says, those who suffer this kind of foolishness "[draw] near the gates of death."

The apostle Paul reiterates this truth: "Do not be deceived. God cannot be mocked. A man reaps what he sows. Whoever sows to please their flesh, from the flesh will reap destruction; whoever sows to please the Spirit, from the Spirit will reap eternal life" (Galatians 6:7-8). Thankfully, we can cry to the Lord in the trouble we've created through our foolish pattern. In the psalmist's third vignette, God "sent out his word and healed them; he rescued them from the grave" (Psalm 107:20).

If you've ever suffered from your own poor choices; if you've ever felt regret pressing into you like a weight that's almost too heavy to carry; if you've ever felt you have no choice but to live forever with the pain of past decisions, then you know what this kind of affliction feels like. Psalm 31:7 says, "I will be glad and rejoice in your love, for you saw my affliction and knew the anguish of my soul." Jesus said, "It is not the healthy who need a doctor, but the sick. I have not come to call the righteous, but sinners" (Mark 2:17).

If you relate to this account of affliction, there is good news. Jesus has you in His sights. You are His target. He came to give you—yes, you—a new life. For those who can accept the reality therapy of their own foolishness, this word from Jesus is an incredible proposition: "Whoever loses their life for me will find it" (Matthew 16:25).

Is healing your story?

Story Theme #4: Overwhelmed

Some people do not wander off intentionally but find themselves overwhelmed by a life they thought would satisfy. In Psalm 107, this fourth vignette is about the power brokers of the day—the merchants in ships, the pioneers of the mighty waters. As they ventured out into the sea, they "saw the works of the Lord . . . for he spoke and stirred up a tempest" (verses 24-25). The psalmist uses the Hebrew words *amar* and *ruah*, the same words used to describe God speaking (*amar*) the world into creation, breathing (*ruah*) life into the world in Genesis 1.

Here, God used that same creative power to breathe a storm into being, which melted the courage of the merchants and led them to "their wits' end" (verse 27), or literally "their *wisdom's* end." In this story theme, strong people were intentionally brought to the end of their wisdom by God's all-surpassing strength and power. The storm rushed in, and they were reminded of their fragile and weak state. It was only then that they cried out to God for help, and He "stilled the storm to a whisper; the waves of the sea were hushed . . . and he guided them to their desired haven" (verses 29-30).

In the Gospel of Luke, we read of a time when Jesus'

disciples experienced this story theme in full and blasting reality. When they were in a boat with Jesus, a huge and sudden storm swept down on the lake (Luke 8:23). Matthew tells this same story, and he says the storm came up "without warning" (Matthew 8:24). Jesus' disciples, many of them career fishermen, were terrified, and rightfully so. Each account says the storm put them in great danger and they were almost swamped. This was a worst-case scenario for these skilled boatsmen who knew the true power and strength of the sea. The disciples then did what I think any of us would do: They woke up the boss, who'd been sleeping in the back of the boat. "Master, Master, we're going to drown!" (Luke 8:24). In Psalm 107, the "overwhelmed" story theme is poetic. In this Gospel story, it's a salt-water-in-your-throat reality. These disciples embodied the exact story of the psalm—their courage melted away, and they were at their own wisdom's end.

Now here's where the story gets astonishing. Jesus woke up from His nap in the back of the boat and spoke. In the accounts in Matthew, Mark, and Luke, the writers use the same word to describe Jesus' relationship with the sea. He rebuked it, which would be our modern-day equivalent of a sharp correction, a sort of "shut up!" to the blasting wind and raging waters. Imagine yourself in this kind of perilous situation. I don't know if you've ever been in real danger, the kind of physical insecurity where you aren't sure if there will be any way out, but if you have, you know the overwhelming realization of your own fragility as a human being. Into that kind of situation, Jesus spoke with one sharp phrase and *all was calm.* The wind stopped howling, the waves stopped screaming, and there was nothing but complete calm.

Power is a clarifying agent. When we are in that kind of storm, we know our own weaknesses. But storms also know their own limitations compared to the all-surpassing power of God. The very breath that can bring a storm into being can also calm it into submission with just a word.

Your own story might not have an element of physical danger to it, but maybe you know the kind of storms that happen on the inside—the raging fear, the powerful doubts, the tumultuous history. Perhaps you are well-acquainted with the sense that your plans to live a meaningful life have been waylaid by the power of things you cannot control. Maybe you've had that moment of coming to your own wisdom's end and crying out to God, asking Him to still that storm in your life. It might not have happened all at once—but you've known what it is to find safe haven in God. Sometimes we don't recognize the stronghold of God's presence until after the fact, until we trace the map lines back in our stories and see that place of power.

Is finding refuge your story?

The New Story Line

Whether you resonate with one of the four words or with different elements of each, these themes from Psalm 107 all point to the power of the redemptive story line. Psalm 107:2 says, "Let the *redeemed* of the LORD tell their story" (emphasis added). A redemptive story line is possible once we recognize our brokenness and inability to fix our issues. Amazingly, it is only at this point of helplessness that we discover Christ's love.

When Jesus Christ entered the world in all the humility of a baby, in all the modesty of a poor Jewish family, in all the normalcy of humanity, He didn't just teach a new way of living. He didn't just show a new way of living either. He crushed the dividing line between God and our broken selves with an entirely new promise of life in Him. He became the turning point in every story, whether it was an account of being lost, bound, afflicted, or overwhelmed. He came to find our lost hearts. He came to set us free from the power of sin and death. He came to heal us from every soul disease. He came to be our captain in the winds and waves of life. When we tell our stories through this lens, we begin to find the redeeming power of Christ. We look back and find those places where we thought He wasn't present, where we have wondered if He missed us or abandoned us. And we learn that He has the power to rewrite those chapters and reframe the plot. Psalm 107 ends with, "Those who are wise will take all this to heart; they will see in our history the faithful love of the LORD" (verse 43, NLT).

Madeleine L'Engle wrote, "Stories are able to help us to become more whole, to become Named. And Naming is one of the impulses behind all art; to give a name to the cosmos we see despite all the chaos."[3] When Jesus becomes the center of our stories, the stories become different. We become different.

Remember the Perm Incident of '89? When I got that perm, I lost some innocence. The shadow of brokenness that had brushed my life became real, and I saw people for who they really could be—cruel, mocking, merciless. I put that story away for a decade and never spoke of it because when you move around your whole childhood, you can reinvent yourself and lock pain away pretty easily.

My hair eventually became straight again, but the moment had left its mark. I struggled with the story of what really matters throughout my teenage and early adult years. I could trace back and find moment after moment where I kept living the lies that *people are cruel* and *you have to fend for yourself* and *be perfect to avoid hurt*. Slowly but surely, Jesus began to break into my own lost story with His truth. The unraveling of the old story happened through new relationships, the love of my boyfriend-turned-husband, and the warmth and love of God. I had tried to stitch up my own wounds, but the Great Healer was not satisfied with my clumsy efforts.

Ten years after the Perm Incident and what felt like a lifetime later, I sat in a circle of preteen girls in the middle of a high school cafeteria. Their knees were bony, their hair was frizzy, and their smiles were all flashes of metal and rubber bands. Some were pudgy in the middle, and some were too tall for their jeans. They sat hunched over, mostly, like they were trying not to be women yet. I was twenty-two and in the middle of my own personal crisis, a whirlwind of emotions that come with trying to be a grown-up, trying to be a wife, trying to be a person of any kind of substance, and feeling as if I were failing miserably. But I was in a little church plant, and I was experiencing this strong and loving presence of grace in that place. Our church, aptly named Hope, met Sundays in that high school, and I was charged with the spiritual care and keeping of these middle school girls. And so in that circle of bony knees and insecurity, I found myself telling them about the Perm Incident.

I had never told anyone about that perm until that day—not the real story, anyway. But something about the girls' innocent and open faces made me become more honest, and maybe more hopeful. I told them the unvarnished truth about the half bathroom and the dismay of hating what I saw in the mirror. I told them about the results and the bullying from Doug and how I cried night after night. And I told them that it was okay if they felt ugly or unsure, because that was not how God saw them. I told them they were God's masterpieces, works in progress, and it was okay because, hey, I made it all the way to twenty-two. I survived the perm and the boy and the teasing and *look here, I can laugh about it.*

What they didn't know was that I was laughing about it for the very first time. In that moment, I opened a closed door of my story because a preteen girl just like the one I used to be needed that door opened. What I expected was that same preteen pain to be on the other side of the door, waiting for me right where I had left it. But surprise . . . what I got instead was joy. Where there had been bondage, there was now freedom. It turns out that Jesus was the One who had opened that door, who had been right there with me at age twelve when it happened and was still with me at twenty-two when I retold it. He was waiting right there to transfigure the story with His grace.

When I look back on that day, I mark it as the beginning of the end of the old story. The freedom that came from my honesty was exhilarating, wild, and wonderful. Over time, every other door that was locked began to open. Some of the doors housed much more painful memories than the perm. Some of them took time and prayer and some years to unravel and rethread into the new story, the redeemed story, the story where Jesus has never left me or forsaken me; where His resurrection power can bring even the dead stuff in me back to life; where every foolish and weak and shameful thing becomes a place of His glory and presence. The new story is written in God's wisdom, full of His grace, overflowing with His love. The new story gives me the freedom to walk forward, casting off the "reap and sow" mentality of the old life.

Yes, it's true: "GOD rewrote the text of my life when I opened the book of my heart to his eyes."[4] And He'll rewrite yours, too.

Keeping It Real

1. When you consider Psalm 107's four story themes—lost, bound, afflicted, overwhelmed—can you find yourself in one or more of them? Explain.

2. Have you experienced a "rewritten" version of an old pain in your life? How did that happen?

3. Are there parts of your story that still feel dis-integrated into your life? What is keeping you from embracing all of your story?

Living Into the New and True Story

If you are thinking, *This whole new story thing is too good to be true,* believe me, I understand. I spent years thinking the idea that I could change my everyday life simply by knowing and believing the Bible was ridiculous. I thought my kind of struggle was somehow both too easy for God (*Why would God care about my car not passing inspection?*) and too hard for God (*Nothing and no one can change my feelings about this situation*). So if you've had similar thoughts, you are not alone! It takes faith to stick with our ground rule: *God is greatest, and He knows best.* When I wondered whether the Bible could change anything, I realized my real struggle was with God—did the Lord of the universe really care? And care about me? If so, how could I experience His care in my daily life? How did knowing God's wisdom impact the people, the places, and the challenges I faced every single day?

If you have those questions—if you've been afraid that nothing can really change and that the Struggle will always be the same; if you think, *Yeah, that sounds great, but it's never worked for me*—then we are about to get to the real work of learning how to live from your new story. Now that we've laid the foundation to help you see why you can and should believe in a better story, we are actually going to do the work of revising that story in God's wisdom.

We are going to take all of this—the truth about our struggles now and our struggles in the past—and reconcile it into the new story. We are going to do it by God's form of reality therapy: through relentless honesty and courageous faith. Here are the essential elements for your new story: First, we are going to understand how to find and live within the freedom cycle. Second, we will look together at how to listen for God's voice in your new story. Next, we'll cover three story lines that we all need to reckon with: recognizing how our stories have been shaped by our families, understanding how we shape our stories with the words we use, and paying attention to times of transition and loss that we will all face.

The progress you'll make will not necessarily be linear—one area may be more timely than another. I can't predict how God is working in your life, but I am confident that He *is* working! As we explore these foundational elements together, I believe God will surprise you with His abundant ability to replace pain with joy, to move mountains of regret into spacious places of freedom, and to bring clarity where there has been confusion.

Author Beth Moore says, "Profound works of God that take place in us and that take place through us don't come overnight."[1] I think that's what it means when Scripture tells us to "continue to work out your salvation with fear and trembling" (Philippians 2:12). There is a once-and-for-all-time nature to our relationship in God, but then there is the process of "working out" what it means to live into our new stories. So let's work it out together.

6

The Rewrite
Follow the Freedom Cycle

It is no small pity, and should cause us no little
shame, that, through our own fault, we do not
understand ourselves, or know who we are.

ST. TERESA OF AVILA

I don't like to brag, but I think I might be better than 99 percent of the population at one particular skill: braiding hair. I can fishtail, rope, and French braid. I can waterfall and even do the upside-down braid. Thanks to the double French braids required of my high school cheerleading squad and then as the mom of a gymnastics-loving daughter, I am confident in my braids. I can whip braids out of the most unruly hair. Curly, thick, thin, short—if my subject has a high pain tolerance and some patience, I will get a magnificent braid out of even the most stubborn head.

Because I might be the best hair-braiding mom in my

neighborhood, you might assume I excel at other crafty endeavors requiring hand dexterity and spatial perception.

You would be wrong.

My point: There's a difference between perfecting one skill that by some broad and generous definition might be considered crafty, and being a "crafty" person. And by crafty person, I mean: "Look at the sixty-seven hair bows I whipped together for my daughter's dance team last night!" Crafty as in "Check out the coffee table I built over the weekend using only a dumpster pallet and mason jars!"

Living into my one crafty skill does not make me a crafty person. Artsy-craftsy people can make magic out of what appears to be trash. They just exude creativity. You see it everywhere—in their homes, in the food they whip up, in the gifts they make. I don't even know how to find a whale-shaped birthday cake on Pinterest, much less actually make one. A crafty person is the one who came up with the recipe and then posted it on Pinterest with step-by-step pictures that use words like *just* as in "just shape the whale mold out of leftover cereal boxes" and *simply* as in "simply assemble the whale head using dowel rods and your favorite fondant recipe." There is nothing "just" or "simple" about crafts for me. I have one crafty skill, and that's it.

As you begin to uncover your new story, it's important you realize that God isn't calling you to develop a certain skill or to alter one behavior. He is inviting you to a change of mind. He is leading you to a transformation of your heart and a shift in how you see your relationships, your struggles, and your future. He is seeking a change of attitude and a change of patterns—the well-grooved ways of thinking, reacting, and interpreting your world. The bottom line? God wants it all. He wants to transform you in the deepest place so that you experience a comprehensive transformation. The oft-quoted verse "If anyone is in Christ, he is a new creation" (2 Corinthians 5:17, ESV) is a real invitation to each and every one of us.

If you are going to live deliberately into the life God has for you, you will begin to exhibit different attitudes and patterns when it comes to all four of your major relationships— your relationship with God, yourself, others, and the world. You will not embrace the forgiveness God has given you without actually becoming more forgiving toward yourself and others. You will not begin to love God more wholeheartedly without also beginning to be more loving toward others. As you learn to resolve the Struggle and live into your new story, you will experience a wholehearted change that will affect all your relationships, not just one.

You may argue that you are growing in your relationship with God but still struggling when relating with other people. I would tell you in the kindest tone possible that if that continues to be the case over time—if you feel as if you know God but continue to harbor resentment, bitterness, and intolerance in your heart toward those with whom you struggle in life—I do not think you are growing in God.

This is in *no way* a condemnation of you or a judgment on your salvation. This is not a call to more "works" to prove that you are loved by God. It is merely a statement of fact

When you experience true transformation in your spirit, you will experience that transformation across all relationships. that is supported by Scripture and by all the psychological literature on what it means to be a healthy person. It is a rule of the universe that when you experience true transformation in your spirit, you will experience that transformation in every relationship. Scripture shows how you can measure this in all four key areas.

Transformed in your relationship with God:

I love those who love me,
    and those who seek me find me.
PROVERBS 8:17

Transformed in your relationship with yourself:

To acquire wisdom is to love yourself;
    people who cherish understanding will prosper.
PROVERBS 19:8, NLT

Transformed in your relationships with others:

If someone says, "I love God," but hates a fellow believer, that person is a liar; for if we don't love people we can see, how can we love God, whom we cannot see?
1 JOHN 4:20, NLT

Transformed in your relationship with the world:

> Pure and genuine religion in the sight of God the
> Father means caring for orphans and widows in their
> distress and refusing to let the world corrupt you.
>
> JAMES 1:27, NLT

My deepest desire is that this talk of transformation does
not live in a Sunday school category in your soul, because
Jesus didn't teach Sunday school. He taught about the good
life for every human condition. He taught about the sin
and struggle in each of us and how to find life to the full—
to "lose" our lives as they were and find the life He offers
(John 10:10; Matthew 10:39). So Jesus is really teaching
Life school—for every day, for every circumstance, for every
relationship.

If I had to choose one word that encapsulates what a
completely transformed life looks like, it would be *freedom*:
the freedom to be generous with your stuff, your kindness,
and your forgiveness. The freedom to be fully, authentically
yourself. The freedom to experience the world as a place of
wonder and to feel a sense of meaning and purpose throughout your life.

Have you ever watched a toddler who was completely
unencumbered with herself? I have a little three-year-old
friend named Myla. She sings when she feels like singing.
She dances when she wants to dance. She tells me the truth,
unfiltered, all the time. She gets excited about important
things, like friends, dogs, and cake. Especially cake. Myla is

a living picture of freedom. Freedom is critical to developing wisdom because true growth happens only in an environment of freedom. We know that shame doesn't work. Rules don't work. Gritting our teeth harder doesn't work. The only way into our transfigured stories is by living in the freedom that God gives us.

The Freedom Cycle

Remember the analogy of crafts and craftiness? As silly as it might be, one reason I use it is to illustrate the difference between the action and the essence of a person. Actions are circumstantial; essence is universal. Actions change; essence doesn't. So when we consider our relationship to God and what it means to live in His freedom, it's important that we understand His essence and how that impacts our relationship with Him.

Perhaps you are familiar with the story in the Bible of the woman whose actions get her caught in a compromising situation with a man—and in big trouble. We pick up the account the moment her problems are going from bad to worse—not only is she in a mess, but she's been caught by some powerful people with the ability to ruin her life—perhaps even *take* her life. In fact, her accusers bring her before a crowd that has gathered to listen to a wise teacher. Suddenly, these self-appointed prosecutors make her private situation very public. She is now an object lesson, forced to the front of the crowd to illustrate a point.

As she stands there, her accusers ask the teacher a question, one related to a legal matter and the punishment she deserves. They don't call the woman by her name but simply refer to her by her sin—adultery. Clearly her powerful accusers see her as an object, a pawn to be used in a bigger power struggle.

Curiously, the teacher listens and then bends down and begins to write on the ground, right in this moment of tension. But the accusers are not distracted—they just demand that He answer their question. So He stands up with an unexpected proposal: that whoever among them is free of any trouble or sin—well, that person should be the first to throw a stone, as the law of Moses requires.

After that, the teacher crouches again and resumes writing on the ground. Slowly the crowd disperses—one by one and one at a time, the older ones first. Before long, no one is left. Not one of the powerful people. Not one person from the crowd of onlookers. No one but the one wise man and the one troublesome woman.

In this story of the Pharisees confronting the sinful woman—and ultimately, Jesus—wisdom intersects with ordinary. The ordinary, messy, and profane parts of the world come together before the person of Jesus, and we get this brief and bright window into the nature of God. The story (you can read it for yourself in John 8:2-11) gives no hint that this woman is contrite or even humbled by her sin. Heck, we have no way of knowing whether she even believes that what she did is sin! We might assume she feels shame, but the story does not specifically bring her guilt into the picture. I wonder if none of her words or emotions are recorded in order to magnify the reality that her action—or reaction—has no bearing on the wisdom of Jesus. He doesn't respond to her because of something she's done or said. He responds to her on the basis of His character, not hers.

Once Jesus is alone with the woman, He asks her, "Has no one condemned you?" Looking into those eyes of grace, love, and freedom, the woman replies: "No one, sir." And He says, "Neither do I condemn you. Go now and leave your life of sin."

Jesus is calling this woman into a different life, a different story—something possible once Jesus declares that she is not under condemnation. This story reflects something crucial about God's nature, reflected in His Son. He offers us love, truth, forgiveness, and freedom. These virtues are not circumstantial. They are part of His essence. They are for you when you believe and for you when you don't. And when you live knowing God in this way, you live in a constant state of both love *and* truth, of both acceptance *and* growth.

Because it's so foreign to us in our broken state, I don't know if I can stress enough that the freedom Jesus offers is not based on what we do or how worthy we are. The good news is that this freedom is based 100 percent on *His* character and 0 percent on *ours*. Jesus said, "Greater love has no one than this: to lay down one's life for one's friends" (John 15:13). Jesus didn't just lay down his life for us when we think we are good enough—because we are never good enough. In fact, it's in the very understanding that we can *never* be good enough that we begin to scratch the surface of just how incredible His love for us is. For no reason other than love, God chose to come in the flesh through Jesus, to walk how we walk, to live how we live, and to give His life as a sacrifice so that we might be in communion with God. This is how we know what love is. This is where our freedom—and the transformation that comes with it—begins.

How do we know that we are experiencing the transformation that comes from living in our new stories? I developed something I call the freedom cycle to illustrate this. The cycle doesn't have a beginning or an end, but it does have a general pattern. Each step bears fruit in our hearts and equips us to pursue God's best every day. It illustrates the practical steps we can take to move toward wise living. It looks like this:

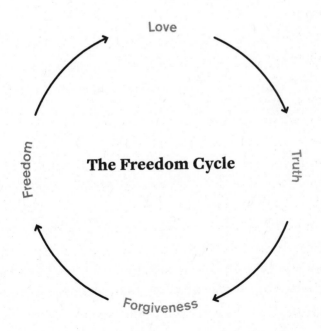

Let's look at each aspect of this cycle to see what it reveals about how you can know if you are living into the new story:

Love

Your understanding of the nature of God starts with His love for you. His love is what set your life into motion. His love for you is what sent Jesus into the world, and His love will outlast everything else. "Now these three remain: faith, hope and love. But the greatest of these is love" (1 Corinthians 13:13).

You know you are living in this love when you experience *security* in your inner world and embrace *vulnerability* about who you really are.

Truth

When you have experienced God's love, you are able to move toward truth. Truth is the rigorous honesty with yourself that allows you to see your broken places and not hide from them. Truth keeps you steadfast in the face of sin, allowing the Holy Spirit to reveal to you who you really are. Truth allows you to see others as they really are as well. "When he, the Spirit of truth, comes, he will guide you into all truth" (John 16:13).

You know you are living in truth when you experience a deep desire for *wholeness* coupled with recognition of your *helplessness* to fix yourself. You understand that healing comes only from Christ, not from anything you can do within.

Forgiveness

Experiencing love and embracing truth will always lead you to desire forgiveness. Forgiveness is the act of allowing the truth of what you've thought, felt, or done to be made right through the sacrifice of Christ. The Bible tells us that Christ took the charges against us and canceled them by nailing them to the cross with His sacrifice.

Your forgiveness is based on the character of Christ, who is always faithful and always just. Christ made this forgiveness possible with His own body and His own blood. All you need to do is come to the table. "If we confess our sins, he is faithful and just and will forgive us our sins and purify us from all unrighteousness" (1 John 1:9).

You know you are living in forgiveness when you experience a sense of *healing* and *transformation*.

Freedom

Through the process of accepting love, receiving truth, and seeking forgiveness, you are freed to be fully yourself. The agreements you've made about who you are in the world begin to be undone. Your soul begins to expand with joy and peace. Christ in you increases; fear and insecurity decrease. "Where the Spirit of the Lord is, there is freedom" (2 Corinthians 3:17).

You know you are living in freedom when your overall sense of *gratitude* in life and *compassion* for yourself and others increase.

As you live out the love-truth-forgiveness-freedom cycle, you find that you are not just becoming a person who performs more Christlike actions; you actually *become* more Christlike. The move toward freedom is a metamorphosis of the soul that slowly, almost imperceptibly, begins to rewrite your life story. You understand that your wrongs do not cancel your rights because you are safe and secure in the righteousness of Christ. In the new story, freedom and security give you the room to grow. To see your past hurts differently. To confront present struggles with compassion and courage. To embrace the future with trust and joy. You don't become someone who just does wise things. You become a wise person.

I know this sounds all well and good on paper, but maybe you wonder how this can actually impact your reality. Let me

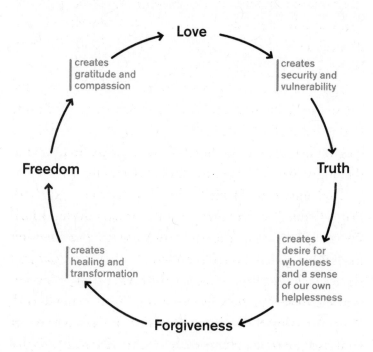

tell you about my friend Danielle, someone I consider a perfect example of how the growth cycle leads us to live in our redeemed stories. Danielle would describe herself as "happily single 90 percent of the time." She's an independent woman who has a vibrant relationship with God, a great community of friends, and a sense of purpose and meaning in her life. But she struggles with the other 10 percent—that part of her that has a deep longing to be loved, to be a mother, to have a soul mate. Because she wants to live in the "happily single" side of herself all the time, she often has a hard time getting honest with the 10 percent of her that's lonely and disappointed. But after a recent series of normal struggles (car trouble, roommate issues, job turmoil) left her painfully aware of how alone she felt, she finally acknowledged that sliver of dissatisfaction and cried out to God from the most honest part of her soul.

Danielle told the Lord about her loneliness, her disappointment, her frustration at her singleness. She had come to that place of good desperation where she had nothing to give but her honesty and humility, where she surrendered to the reality that *God is greatest, and He knows best.*

God answered Danielle, but not as she'd expected. Danielle told me that after a couple of days during which she cried out to God, she had a strong sense, an impression that seemed to come out of nowhere: *You need to forgive your dad.* I laughed when she told me her reaction: She rolled her eyes and looked to the heavens, saying, "God, get on board. We ain't talking about *my dad*!" But try as she might to get God back on topic, He wasn't having it. *You need to forgive your dad* kept coming to her mind. Sometimes we recognize God's voice in the statement that we do *not* want to hear but that we also realize is in line with what God wants for us based on what we know from His Word. Since the essence of God is forgiveness, He wants His children to fully know the freedom of forgiveness.

Danielle's cycle of growth began when she finally accepted God's prompting as an absolute truth she needed to address. The first step was the hardest—she had to acknowledge that she had really been hurt by her dad and actually hadn't forgiven him. It's easy as Christians to lump all forgiveness together and think, *Of course I've forgiven my dad [or mom/sister/ex-boyfriend/classmate].* We may have forgiven someone intellectually, but that doesn't mean that the hurt kid inside of us has actually forgiven him or her. Sometimes to live into our new stories, we have to trace back to a hurtful memory to see the broken kids in our stories, to walk back hand in hand with Jesus and meet those kids right where we left them, to walk them through that painful place and into the spacious place where they are safe, loved, and accepted in Christ.

The opportunity to walk back in our stories with Jesus might present itself when a snapshot of a memory comes to mind and we invite Him to connect the way we feel today to any hurt from our past. It might mean taking an honest feeling (insecurity, anger, resentment, powerlessness) into God's presence and allowing Him to uncover, rewrite, and release us from the power of a memory or pattern in our past.

As Danielle allowed memories to come to mind, she saw

her childhood through adult eyes. She saw that her police officer dad was often sharp and domineering in his requests, yet distant and guarded in his affection. She brought it all before God in the next few weeks, journaling through memories of times when her dad had let her down. She didn't try to make sense of it herself. Instead she came to her heavenly Father—just like a kid might go to her dad—with a confusing situation she couldn't sort out herself and with powerful feelings she couldn't release herself. She just expressed her broken story with rigorous honesty, and that's when God broke in with all kinds of reminders. For the first time, Danielle was prompted to think about the dad who raised *her* dad. She realized that her father's brokenness didn't start with him but began generations before. She felt a strange new warmth toward her dad as God reminded her that only He was her perfect Father who wanted to meet all the needs her earthly dad couldn't.

"And then the craziest thing happened," Danielle told me. "As I acknowledged all the ways my dad hurt me, but also the ways I know he's been hurt, our relationship changed. I stopped feeling like I had this underground current of things I needed him to be. I stopped needing him to be anyone except who he was. It was like all of a sudden, the pressure was off our relationship."

Because of Danielle's confidence in God's love for her and her willingness to filter hard memories through His lens, the Lord began to rewrite her story and walk her through the growth cycle. She began by recognizing the truth (about all of her feelings, not just the 90 percent she liked) and recognizing her need to forgive both her dad and herself (for her own hardness of heart toward him). As she opened her heart to forgive and understand her dad, she experienced transformation as God began to heal her. She didn't make a big announcement to her dad or engage in a big heart-to-heart discussion with him. She just felt freedom—and in feeling that freedom, she began to interact with her dad differently. She felt the freedom to let him off the hook, and then she discovered she could appreciate him for who he really is—broken, yes, but also a man *trying* to love her as best he knew how. It took a vigilant mind-set not to slip back into the resentment she had felt toward her dad, so she sought out the passages in the Bible that talk about God's role as our heavenly Father. She read them over and over until she started to really believe them, and while she wasn't even paying attention to her dad, her love for him changed. By fixing her eyes on Jesus, Jesus took care of what she had been fixated on.

This story isn't over—Danielle is still happily single 90 percent of the time. Forgiving her father didn't immediately bring Prince Charming on the scene (hopefully we all know that God doesn't work like that), but it did bring her life-giving healing and growth. Danielle is growing in compassion even as she continues to struggle. She's growing in her trust in God. She's growing in wisdom through the struggle, rather than letting that struggle continue to create a festering place of resentment and strife in her soul. For Danielle, the struggle has been real, and it's also proven itself good.

Derailers

This all looks easy when it's described on paper, but when it comes to our hearts—well, that's complicated. I've learned from personal experience that, even after making progress on the freedom cycle, we will inevitably make unplanned detours off the path. Just the other night I was scrubbing the kitchen counters for what felt like the hundredth time that day, cleaning up behind my darling kids who keep getting bigger and whose messes keep growing with them. As I scrubbed at egg yolk spilled at seven o'clock that morning, I called out to my husband in the other room, punctuating my words with the efforts of my fierce scrubbing: "I don't know why our children act the way that they do. I don't want us raising entitled kids. How can they sit by and watch me slave over them in the kitchen and not raise a finger to help? And then there's the attitude! I can't stand that attitude of injustice, as if I'm not handing them *every single thing* they have! I offer one correction, and I get the eye roll as they stomp out of the room!"

I'll spare you the rest of my rant, but it continued in exactly that manner. I came up for air as I finally dislodged the egg yolk. Just then my husband yelled from the couch, "Are you talking to me?"

"Yes, I'm talking to you!"

He replied, "Oh, sorry, wasn't listening! What's up?"

In the seconds it took for him to answer me with kindness, I realized how fiery and acrid my passionate monologue had been. And because I was writing this chapter, the next thought that came knocking on the door of my heart was this one: *How does the freedom cycle matter right now?*

You see, it's often easier to diagnose what's going on in our hearts by what's *not* going right than by what is. And when it comes to the freedom cycle, there are places where we derail all the time. If we aren't experiencing all of God's character, then we quickly veer off. If we know God's love but we don't know His truth, that's a problem. If we know His forgiveness but don't move toward freedom, that's a problem. There is not one element in the cycle that we can bypass and still know the fullness of God, or His essence. Just as you can't be fully known by someone who refuses to recognize important elements in your personality, so we can't know God in His fullness if we don't acknowledge all aspects of His being.

> *It's often easier to diagnose what's going on in our hearts by what's* **not going right** *than by what is.*

And freedom derailers are a sign that we are missing out on an aspect of God's goodness. Think of these derailers as off-ramps on the freedom cycle, where instead of embracing the next aspect of God, we accidentally head a different way.

It's in our daily living—in the moments when we stop to listen to our frustration, disappointment, and confusion—that we recognize our freedom cycle derailers.

Love derailers: If you embrace God's love but don't let it lead you to rigorous truth about your broken story and the broken-storied people around you, you will off-ramp into licentiousness and hypocrisy. God's love without God's truth will give you a distorted view of yourself and others. You might assume, as the Pharisees did, that you are superior to someone else: "If we claim to be without sin, we deceive ourselves and the truth is not in us" (1 John 1:8).

Truth derailers: If you reckon with the truth but don't desire forgiveness and extend it to others, you will off-ramp into denying who you really are. "People who conceal their sins will not prosper, but if they confess and turn from them, they will receive mercy" (Proverbs 28:13, NLT). Blaming those you believe "made" you the way you are will also lead you to diverge from the freedom cycle. Remember how Danielle initially resisted God's prompting that she consider her attitude toward her dad? If she had refused to obey, she would have derailed as well: "Do not be overcome by evil, but overcome evil with good" (Romans 12:21).

Forgiveness derailers: If you experience forgiveness but do not accept the freedom that comes with it, your off-ramp will lead you into guilt and shame. You will stay in a perpetual cycle of whipping yourself with your former sins, always beaten—never victorious. When you derail here, you continue to live under the weight of your sin, doubting God's ability to actually forgive you, not believing that "as far as the east is from the west, so far has he removed our transgressions from us" (Psalm 103:12). This derailment will cause you to struggle with God's promise that "those who trust in me will never be put to shame" (Isaiah 49:23, NLT).

Freedom derailers: If you live in God's freedom but don't allow His love to shape your freedom, you will detour into pride and foolishness. You will use His freedom to justify your own actions, rather than letting that freedom lead you into deeper, sacrificial love. "If you love me, obey my commandments" (John 14:15, NLT).

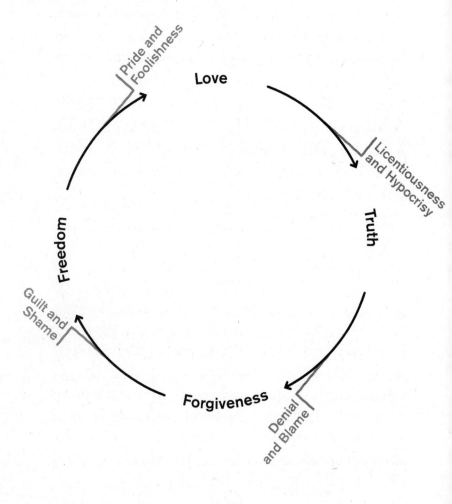

Most of us are more tempted by certain off-ramps than by others. Those bypasses are probably well-worn from the many times we've veered off course from God's goodness. These worn grooves in our souls can be hard to break without an intentional effort. This is where the reality check of "choose your hard" comes into play. Which problem would you rather have? Would you rather focus on the shortcomings of others than acknowledge the sin in your own heart, leading to a false sense of your superiority? Would you prefer to continue down the road of negativity and blame, or passionately seek God's freedom in your life? Would you rather continue to guard and deny the truth than allow the Healer to do His work by revealing what's really going on inside you?

When you find that you've taken an off-ramp away from the freedom cycle, the only way to get back on track is to identify the aspect of God's essence that you've missed. Is it His love, unrelenting and faithful? Is it His truth, where He meets you with the full knowledge of your broken places and woos you to believe in your new story? Is it His forgiveness, where He delights in putting you back on your feet over and over again? Is it His freedom, where gratitude and purpose and confidence flow freely from Him into you, so that you can move forward into all the plans He has already set in place for your life? Wherever you find the bitter fruit of living outside of the freedom cycle, you'll find a place where God is calling you to know His goodness and grace more fully.

When I stood at that kitchen counter and ranted about my kids to my not-listening husband (I'm actually kind of glad he wasn't paying attention), God asked me, *What does the freedom cycle say about this?* I thought about it for a while and recognized my derailer: I was living in God's freedom but not moving toward God's love. Although I knew His freedom for myself, I was not allowing that freedom to move me to action in that moment of anger. God's love is sacrificial and humble. God's love moves toward wrongs, not away from them. God calls us to sacrifice, humility, and mature, bold, wide-open love. Because I wanted to move away from my children (preferably to a place with warm sand and cool drinks, but I digress . . .) rather than toward them, my off-ramp in the growth cycle was my own pride.

The freedom cycle always stretches our hearts— sometimes painfully, sometimes gloriously— into the new story that God invites us to write with Him.

At the end of a long day, I was weary and tired of reminding my kids to clean up after themselves. But when I sensed God's voice, I sighed and thanked Him for the conviction because I really do want to grow in the Lord. I really do want to experience Him for myself each and every day. Sometimes that comes through a moment of light and wonder and peace. And sometimes it comes from a little kick in the pants urging me to be the loving person He has made me to be, if I can just get over myself.

I walked into the yolk-dripping child's room and sat on the edge of the bed. I asked some questions about how this one was feeling. I made amends. I moved toward the hurt instead of away from it. The kid softened. I softened. This is what the freedom cycle looks like. It's measured in the inches we move toward one another. It's measured in the moments in which we crucify our own desire to be right all the time and exchange our petty grievances for the goodness and graciousness of God. The freedom cycle always stretches our hearts—sometimes painfully, sometimes gloriously—into the new story that God invites us to write with Him.

Keeping It Real

1. When you consider the freedom cycle, what aspect of God's character is easiest for you to accept? Hardest?

2. Think back over the struggles of the last week. Where are you likely to derail from the freedom cycle?

7

The Listening
Hearing the New Story

Few people arise in the morning
as hungry for God as they are for
cornflakes or toast and eggs.

DALLAS WILLARD

Like any family, ours has its share of dysfunction. We run at a pretty high torque when it comes to perceived slights, unjust chore schedules, and all manner of competition. As my husband and I tell our friends, "Two type A people don't breed laid-back children." Add to that high-intensity environment a tendency toward communication issues, and the struggle gets very real.

We recently moved into a ranch-style home, and the kids' bedrooms are far from the main living space. Sane people would recognize that such distance means it will be hard to hear our children if they try transmitting their messages down a mile-long hallway. Not me. I'll be in the kitchen and hear a muffled cry coming from the other end of the house. Rather than walking toward the child and using my gentle, sincere, wise-living tone, I'll just yell back based on the last few syllables I heard:

"WHAT? YES, GRANDMA'S ON A CRUISE!"

Muffled phrase repeated, more insistently this time.

"WHAT? CLEAR EYES CAN'T LOSE?"

Faint crying of phrase a third time.

Running out of patience, I shout: *"IF YOU NEED ME, COME TO ME!"*

Now type A child sprints down the hallway like a ticking bomb needing to be defused.

In a voice that is breathless, frantic, tearful, and insistent all at once, my child says, "Mom, I can't find my shoes!"

Maybe you can relate. Clear and accurate communication is challenging for all of us, whether in our families, in our own heads, or in the way we communicate with God. Because each of our Struggles is related to the disconnect between what we believe and how we act, between our understanding of the promises of God and our actual experience with Him, honest and trusted conversation with Him is essential. Without it, we will never overcome the chasm between who we are and who we were created to be.

Living into our rewritten stories requires hearing the one true Voice that can take us there. We need to know *how* we can embrace the freedom cycle for our lives. And we need specific direction—in those sticky situations at work, in the way we handle our emotions, in the fears that keep popping up in our souls like rabid prairie dogs. If it's truly hard to communicate well with people we can see, no wonder it can feel hard with an all-powerful God we can't see!

One of the troubling misperceptions among many Christians is that once we are adults, we should have our relationship with God all figured out. My experiences in my own life and with people in the church tell me that this impression is wrong. As my friend AJ says, "A lot of people say they know a lot about Jesus, but they don't actually *know* Jesus." Most people I talk with aren't sure how to hear from God. Many don't read their Bibles regularly because they find it overwhelming and confusing. They really do want to seek God but aren't exactly sure how Scripture is relevant to their busy and somewhat stressful lives. And because it doesn't come easily (we've already covered that), it feels like another item in an endless list of to-dos. No wonder we experience so little life, joy, and transformation.

Friends, this is a tragedy. It is a tragedy to feel as if knowing or hearing from God is just another hard task on our list. If you've felt this way, know that you are not alone. The reason our lack of communication with God is problematic isn't because we don't have it all together or need to be better Christians. It's tragic because hearing from God is our very source of life. He is the One who will guide us into our new stories, which center around who He created us to be and what He planned for us to do as His Kingdom comes.

Author Anne Lamott puts it this way:

There's a lot to be said for having really reached a bottom where you've run out of any more good ideas, or plans for everybody else's behavior; or how to save and fix and rescue; or just get out of a huge mess, possibly of your own creation.

And when you're done, you may take a long, quavering breath and say, "Help." . . . It is the great prayer, and it is the hardest prayer, because you have to admit defeat—you have to surrender, which is the hardest thing any of us do, ever.[1]

Once you experience God as Deliverer, Refuge, and Savior for yourself, all the stories in Scripture become relevant. When you recognize and obey God's voice, you can experience the love, care, power, freedom, and wisdom of your heavenly Father. When the source of all power is talking to you, everything else slides into proper perspective—from life to death, from joy to suffering, from the everyday mundane to the eternally sublime.

There is absolutely no way to experience your struggles differently and grow in wisdom if you do not know how to hear from God. It is impossible to feel deep peace in your decisions if you don't know when you've had a prayer answered. If you have not experienced the gentle but persistent nudge of the Spirit in your soul, how can you have the confidence to live your redeemed story?

Hearing from God and *God hearing from us* are promises repeated in Scripture. People hear from God through a variety of means attested to by Scripture and by the mature believers who have gone before us. And God testifies that He hears us as well:

If my people, who are called by my name, will
humble themselves and pray and seek my face and
turn from their wicked ways, then I will hear from
heaven, and I will forgive their sin and will heal
their land.

2 CHRONICLES 7:14

Then you will call, and the LORD will answer;
you will cry for help, and he will say: Here am I.

ISAIAH 58:9

However, knowing that God will hear you and that you
will hear from God mean nothing if you don't experience this
for yourself. So in this chapter, I'd like to help you understand the basics through a simple outline:

Why you need to hear from God
How you should expect to hear from God
What you can hear from God
When you can hear from God

My hope is that this overview gives you a good launching
point into a conversation with God and into writing your
new story. More practical help is included in the accompany-
ing Bible study and video curriculum. For further reading, I also recommend Dallas Willard's book *Hearing God:
Developing a Conversational Relationship with God*. In his
book, Willard says that "nothing is more central to the practical life of the Christian than confidence in God's individual

dealings with each person."[2] Let's now step back and evaluate the most basic of questions: Why does a human need to hear from God?

Hearing God: The Why

One of the great blessings and curses in my life is my relentless desire to understand the why behind everything. If it's not obvious to you yet, I find human existence to be equal parts beautiful and baffling, with a hefty dose of existential angst mixed in.

Life is full of challenging, frustrating, and mundane experiences, and to live in your new story will require daily, intentional decisions to choose God's design for life and not allow the entropy of a mediocre existence to win the day. Because of that, I never want to waste my time doing anything that doesn't have real purpose or meaning behind it. If I can't understand the why, I'm far less likely to persist in the details when the going gets tough.

When it comes to hearing from God, I think many of us are missing the why behind it, or worse yet, have the wrong why in mind. The idea of God speaking to us may bring with it a sense of foreboding. We feel that if God's attention is fixed on us, it is only because He plans to punish or condemn us. This mixed-up understanding of God is often rooted in our own brokenness, not in our actual experiences with Him. We simply default back to our earthly experiences with power and authority (mothers, fathers, leaders), and our image of God is shaped by the broken image of those people in our lives. Our distant understanding of God creates a distrust and dread of hearing from Him, which only creates more separation.

Some of us distance ourselves from God's voice for a similar reason, but with a twist. We actually like our lives, and we fear that if we open ourselves to God, He may ask something of us that we don't want to do. We try to "fly under the radar," so to speak, hoping to get by in our comfortable lives without bringing too much attention to ourselves. I would suggest that this distance is created by the same distorted view of God—we believe that if we were to hear from God, He would speak a harsh and condemning message rather than a good and beautiful one. In both cases, darkness is at work, actively keeping us away from the glorious light of God's presence.

Jesus quoted the prophet Isaiah when He spoke of people misunderstanding the true nature of God: "For this people's heart has become calloused; they hardly hear with their ears, and they have closed their eyes. Otherwise they might see with their eyes, hear with their ears, understand with their hearts and turn, and I would heal them" (Matthew 13:15).

Understanding God's intent gives us the courage and desire to hear from Him. The more we understand the nature of God (as illustrated in the freedom cycle in chapter 6), the more we will desire true relationship and communion with Him. So *why* do we need to hear from God? Let's look at three truths about God's nature, which illustrate why we will not only want to hear from Him but will desire true, close relationship with Him:

Truth #1: God knows you. He really knows you. God uses the metaphor of a mother with a child to describe the way He understands you. In the book of Isaiah, there is a short passage embedded within a longer poetic reading called the "Servant Songs" that describes the role of Jesus Christ for the future of the world. In this passage, God is answering His people's complaint that He has forgotten about them:

> Zion said, "The LORD has forsaken me,
> the Lord has forgotten me."
> "Can a mother forget the baby at her breast
> and have no compassion on the child she has borne?
> Though she may forget,
> I will not forget you!
> See, I have engraved you on the palms of my hands;
> your walls are ever before me."

ISAIAH 49:14-16

This is not the only place that God uses this metaphor to describe Himself. In Psalm 131, David compares his calm and quiet soul to a "weaned child with its mother" (verse 2). Elsewhere Jesus describes Himself as a mother hen, gathering her chicks underneath her wings.[3]

As a mother, I have an uncanny ability to know things about my children. I have experienced the uneasy sense that bad news was coming before it came. I often can anticipate an illness a couple of days before one of my kids actually becomes sick. And I recognize the distance and hiding in their faces when they have done something they know my husband and I won't like. I cannot explain this way of know-ing them using logical reasoning—it comes from a deeper place, a spiritual place.

This inexplicable "knowing" of a mother about her child is just a shadow of the kind of understanding that God has for each one of us. God knows you in ways that you do not even fully know yourself. He has access to the mystery of you in ways that only He can reveal to you. He understands your broken places, your sinful patterns, and the places that need healing. He heals, frees, and uncovers the truth of you so that you can live with freedom and joy.

Notice that in the Isaiah passage, God tells His people that even in the ways a mother could forget her child, He, as the Creator and ultimate knower of their souls, could never forget them. Everything you know about the powerful ways a mother can understand the ways of her child is magnified in the way God knows you.

Truth #2: God loves you. If you believe God knows you but don't understand His love for you, then you will not want to hear from Him! It's actually quite scary to think about a powerful force that completely knows you but doesn't love you. It brings to mind the work of intelligence agencies that gather information about people to gain power over them. Someone knowing everything about you and not loving you is not a friend—that's an enemy. No wonder you can have underlying fear or concern about hearing from God!

Growing in the belief that God knows you *and* loves you provides the safety for you to relate with Him. As Dallas

Willard notes, "Only our *communion* with God provides the appropriate context for *communications* between us and him."[4]

I think we can spend our whole lives growing in our knowledge of God's love for us. His love is so vast, so deep, so magnificent, and yet so intricate. His love is manifest in the way He has chosen to interact with humans throughout history, culminating in Christ's life, which gave us a living, breathing picture of love. Unfortunately, the word *love* has lost much of its power in our language, as it means all kinds of things. I love coffee, but I also love my work, and I love God. That can confuse us when it comes to understanding the greatest Love, the master key that unlocks the rest.

There is one important distinction between God's love and all the other kinds of loves, and it's this: *God's love is not motivated by needing anything from us.* On some level, all the earthly love we know has some strings attached. There is rarely a moment where there is not give-and-take in a love relationship. My children love me—but they also need me. My friends love me—but they also receive things from me. Yet God needs nothing from us. God is "not served by human hands, as if he needed anything" (Acts 17:25). So if God doesn't need anything from us, why has He done so much to have a relationship with us? The reason must be love. God's love also motivates His desire for us to hear from Him.

Think of it: *God's love is His motivation to know and be known by you.* Really take that in. *His love is His motivation. God's love for you motivates His desire for you to be known by Him and for you to know Him.*

The idea that God knows you and loves you is a powerful combination. Imagine a wise person in your life who knew you 100 percent and loved you 100 percent. You would want to share life and spend time with that person. You would want that person involved in every decision. You would listen to that person—even when offered advice you didn't expect—because you would know that this person knows and loves you completely.

God's love for you motivates His desire for you to be known by Him and for you to know Him.

In the case of your relationship with God, He is not just a wise friend, offering guidance when you ask for it. God is actively seeking a complete relationship with you—as He has throughout all time. He wants to give you "new birth into a living hope" and an inheritance of eternal life with Him and "inexpressible and glorious joy" (1 Peter 1:3-4, 8). You seek to hear from Him because He knows you, loves you, and is actively at work in your world. Not only that, but He calls you to be a part of His work.

Truth #3: God has plans for you. Ephesians 2:10 says that "we are God's workmanship, created in Christ Jesus for good works, which God prepared in advance for us to do." We are not a piece of art to hang on the wall; we are tools in the hand of the Master who is always at work. Jesus said, "My Father is always working, and so am I" (John 5:17, NLT). Not only did God create us for good works, but He prepared those works in advance for us. Before the time line of our lives even began, God had plans for the way He would use our stories. He is actively at work in the world to reconcile and redeem broken people, and He uses new-story people and calls them His church. His church is full of people who know their new story. As a result we can live with freedom that allows us to enjoy communion with God, to move as He directs us, and to be a part of the work that He is always doing. That work is found in its simplest form in the prayer Jesus taught His disciples to pray:

> Your kingdom come,
> your will be done,
>> on earth as it is in heaven.
>
> MATTHEW 6:10

When we pray, "Your kingdom come," the first place His Kingdom will come is in our hearts. When we pray, "Your will be done," the first place His will is expressed is in our hearts. Our hearts change our stories. Our stories change our relationships. And through relationships, one ripple, one generation at a time—the whole world is impacted. Yes, as Jesus promised, "you will be [His] witnesses . . . to the ends of the earth" (Acts 1:8).

So why should you want to hear from God? Because He knows you like no one else does. He loves you beyond your wildest imagination. And He has plans for you as His Kingdom advances throughout the earth.

This might be a good time to pause and consider why you want to hear from God. Are you seeking specific direction from Him? Do you want Him to give you something? If so, those are honest answers, and honesty is the place to start. But I encourage you to think more deeply about the needs underneath your immediate desires. Do you want to be known? Do you need to feel safe? Do you want certainty that you can trust God with your life? Do you want to be truly loved for who you are? Do you want the struggles in your life to make sense? Do you want to wake up each day with a sense of expectation for a grand purpose that God has for your life? Those are the deeper sources of hunger in your soul, and the places that can lead to a new understanding of what it means to hear from God.

Hearing God: The How

So *how* should we expect to hear from God? God will speak to us in three major ways: through His design and purposes (this is what theologians call "general revelation"), through His Word ("specific revelation"), and through our experience of the Holy Spirit.

General revelation is our ability to know God based on His design. If you've ever visited an art exhibit, you know that artwork reveals something about the mind of the artist. If you've followed world-class athletes, you know that people often surmise much about the athletes' performance based on their inner world. Similarly, we know God through the work of His hands. Every time we step outside, we are surrounded by God's artistry. Scripture tells us that the earth is "filled with the knowledge of the glory of the LORD" (Habakkuk 2:14).

The natural world attests to God's character. The paradox of chaos and order found in the microcosm of a little patch of grass; the faithfulness of the cycles of the moon and the cycles of the seasons; the life/death/rebirth of a deciduous tree—all teach us about the nature and glory of God.

The crown of God's creation was man and woman. In His own image He created us. Then He gave us a plan: to be fruitful, to fill the earth, and to subdue it. God gave humankind the ability to be partners in His creation—to bring forth beauty, to lead, and to bring order (to "rule . . . and subdue," Genesis 1:26, 28). We are not passive recipients of God's mercy, living on some kind of spiritual ventilator in the waiting room that is earth, just hoping that heaven isn't too boring. We have been given the high and holy calling to reflect God's image on earth and to actively seek to illuminate the goodness of the Kingdom of God—not tomorrow, not in heaven, but right now, today. On earth. When we are around mature believers who've been seeking God's Kingdom, we see another reflection of God's glory. This is one of the ways our hearts "hear" God.

Specific revelation is the opportunity to know what God is passionate about through the writings that He inspired—the Bible. Although you will not find specific direction on what job to take or what person to marry there, you will find the principles of living in the new and redeemed story of your life. Knowing God's Word allows you to understand what He speaks about and how He speaks. Just like His creation, His Word is varied—He uses story and song, poems and prophets, letters and lists to reveal who He is. Like His creation, His Word is also complex and sometimes mysterious. But over time and with intention, you can begin to recognize His voice in your life because you recognize His character through His Word. Like creation, God's Word is faithful. It's God-breathed and is useful for *thoroughly* equipping you for every good work (2 Timothy 3:16). It doesn't just *sort of* equip you for *some* kinds of work in the *dramatic* seasons of life. It prepares you for every season of life.

The Holy Spirit is the manifestation of God who dwells within you and leads you to truth. The Holy Spirit is the gentle, guiding force that leads you to focus on what God cares about and what He desires. In doing so, your life is shaped to be attentive to the purifying work of God who brings you back into wholeness and glory—your original design, your redeemed story.

Many people are unsure of how the Holy Spirit works in them. Most of us pay too little or too much attention to this member of the Trinity. Too little attention, and we are prone to rely only on common sense and what our logical minds can understand. Too much attention, and we are likely to sway with the winds of our own emotions and overly focus on the "high" of experience rather than on the long, slow, steady work of obedient living. A balanced perspective on the Spirit's work in us might be best summarized by Brother Lawrence in *The Practice of the Presence of God*: "I make it my business only to persevere in His holy presence, wherein I keep myself by a simple attention, and a general fond regard to God."[5]

Some view the Holy Spirit as an internal Magic 8 Ball

toy—helping them decide what to eat for lunch and where to park the car. Scripture documents some instances of the Holy Spirit guiding men and women very specifically, as when the Lord called Ananias in a vision to go to a specific house, ask for a man named Saul, and heal him (Acts 9). Yet the Holy Spirit's guidance is always in line with the work of God's Kingdom, not our comfort or convenience. When we pray for God's direction, we are praying for our desires to be in line with His—which might change our requests altogether. This is what it means to be in a *relationship* with God—to be in communion with Him, to desire what He desires, to interact with His specific words and promises, and to make those promises specific to our requests that God's Kingdom be known in our little grass patch of the world.

Hearing God: The What

Once we know that we will "hear" from God through all of our senses (attentiveness to His creation) as our hearts are open to Him, we also must recognize that God works uniquely in the relationship He has with each of His children. Just as parents do not relate to all of their children in the same way, we can expect that the personal nature of God means our relationship will also have an intimacy unique to each of us. We can also expect that relationship to be ever evolving and growing. How or what God spoke about in our hearts ten years ago may be very different from what He tells us today. After all, maturity and depth of experience come from years of seeking and knowing God. At the same time, we can expect certain patterns of relating to be the same across all people and all time because God's essence and character do not change. For example, God is not gracious to one and condemning to another, for God "wants all people to be saved and to come to a knowledge of the truth" (1 Timothy 2:4).

With this in mind, let's look at three patterns in the ways God will relate to us throughout our lives:

God will remind us to praise Him. Psalm 19 begins with the triumphant truth that "the heavens declare the glory of God; the skies proclaim the work of his hands. Day after day they pour forth speech; night after night they reveal knowledge" (verses 1-2). All around us, God's creation moves us, reminding us to praise our Creator. Scripture repeatedly calls humanity into our greatest act: worshiping God. When we praise God, He does something amazing. When we fix our eyes on Him—when we are not looking at our own problems—He swoops in and heals. When we intentionally turn away from our struggles, He heals the hurt beneath the struggle. When we actively choose to trust Him, He actively works in our lives *even while we rest in Him*. We come into His presence with praise, and we leave His presence with settled, secure hearts, fully at rest and home with our Father in heaven.

Another sign that we were created to praise is our hearts' constant propensity to worship something. If we aren't praising God, we are praising something else. We are warned repeatedly in Scripture to guard our hearts from idols, the created things in our lives that tempt us to praise them. Our worship-hungry hearts will praise many things—be it Christ or ourselves, our ambition, our image.

When we inevitably dethrone God and replace Him with an idol, when we realize that we've made something or someone a higher priority than Him, we have left the freedom cycle. When we submit to His restoring work in our souls by repenting (changing our hearts) and worshiping Him again, we find ourselves back in our new stories. Just as we *dis*-integrate by worshiping created things rather than the Creator, we are restored to wholeness through uninhibited worship. Every time we derail from the freedom cycle, we lose our ability to live in gratitude and praise, and we should expect God's voice to convict us of our sin and bring us back to true worship.

God will direct us into our new stories. In part 1, we talked about the sinister work of the enemy, who takes our memories and actively works to make our brokenness our ultimate truth. He tempts us to believe that something in our truest selves is actually fatally flawed and deeply unworthy.

I have a younger friend who's been a Christian since college. Like all of us, she lives somewhere between the old story and the new. One day when we were together, I could tell she was down. She told me how troubled she felt over some ongoing friction with another friend. "It seems like no matter how much I give, I can never be enough."

The conversation then turned to other places of trouble in her life—her sister's ongoing struggles, the lack of support she felt from her parents, and her general sense of unease that she wasn't doing enough to love the people in her life the way they needed. "I just feel like I'm failing them," she said. With a bit of surprise in her voice, she added, "I guess I think since I'm the one who's a Christian, I need to . . ." Her voice trailed off.

I attempted to finish her sentence, "Do you feel like maybe you need to be perfect . . . so they will know God's love?"

Her eyes filled with tears. "I know that sounds ridiculous. But I guess I do."

When moments like this come, they are sacred. I silently asked God to be present, even though I knew He already was. I gave her a hug. I held her shoulders and looked straight into her eyes. I reminded her that God loved her deeply, and He was not disappointed in her.

I told her that her deep feelings for her friends and family members could go one of two ways. The first way was the old story—driving her to feel guilty and "not enough." The second way was into the new story—where she is troubled for her friends, but she doesn't own their struggles. The second way leads into the new story, where God is on the throne, where He directs her in how to love the people in her life but He does not demand that she save them. In the new story, we are free to be imperfect and limited because we believe that our perfect and limitless God is actually at work. By releasing her misconception that she needed to carry the guilt of being imperfect, my friend could embrace really caring for her friends and family while relying on Christ to love them perfectly.

God reminds us that Jesus' work freed us from the agony

of death—not only our physical death, but also the spiritual death of sin that separates us from ultimate freedom and joy. My friend's good intentions to love her family and friends perfectly was actually a twisted form of pride—an attempt to be "enough" for them without Jesus.

In His gentle and loving way, Christ always brings us back to life. We experience glimpses of that resurrection life in new growth and new hope here on earth. We will experience it completely and finally in heaven, when there will be "no more death or mourning or crying or pain" (Revelation 21:4). In Christ, we no longer live in the old story. That story passed away when we were born again in Christ. Although the victory is already won, we still live in between the stories and will have to intentionally and actively *choose life* every day. God will direct us into the truth of ourselves and the truth of His freedom as He does throughout history and through Scripture.

God will call us to love. Galatians 5:13 says, "You have been called to live in freedom, my brothers and sisters. But don't use your freedom to satisfy your sinful nature. Instead, use your freedom to serve one another in love" (NLT). God frees you from the old story not only for your sake, but for the sake of many who will be impacted by your new-story life. You can expect God to eagerly desire to write you into other people's stories. And the way He does that is by calling you to love them. Love is God's highest priority: "Love the Lord your God with all your heart and with all your soul and with all your mind," said Jesus, calling this "the first and greatest commandment." But he backs it up with the next, which he clarifies is just like the first: "Love your neighbor as yourself" (Matthew 22:37-39).

Your new story will always include an active component of sacrificial love. One of the fruits of wholehearted living is love in your relationships. God is always seeking to deepen your love for others, mostly through the close and sometimes difficult relationships in your story—your family, your neighbors, your coworkers. He's chosen each of these relationships for you.

Dave and I recently got into a heated conversation about how to care for each other. I asserted that I needed romantic and quality time; he insisted that I made it virtually impossible for him to know what that meant, and besides, he felt he was already doing a fine job in that area. As these kinds of conversations usually go for us, we both felt misunderstood at times. There was some dramatic passion (from me) and some logical reasoning (from him), along with some stops and starts in the conversation along the way. Our conversation ended in stony silence. We sat next to each other on the couch, eyes looking straight ahead. As the moments stretched to minutes, I wondered who would make the first move. I was angry, and I'm not good at letting go of being mad when I don't feel heard. It's part of my old story, to always guard and protect, to defend my own rights and protect myself.

So the silence continued. I wanted to reach for the remote between us, aim and fire at the TV, punctuating the silence with a big exclamation point of "And we aren't talking about this for the rest of the night!" But as God often does, He spoke to my heart. It wasn't an audible voice. It wasn't a dream or a vision. It wasn't even a Bible verse. It was a God-intuition. I had read an article earlier in the week that said that intuition is the ability to process multiple facts into a conclusion. I began to process multiple facts about God and myself:

Freedom in Christ means I'm called to love.
Love means not being right all the time.
I'm always the one to hold the grudge.
Maybe it's my turn to make the first move.

The conclusion: My old story is that I'm the one who waits for Dave to move toward me. In that moment, I realized that in our twenty years of marriage, I had rarely (maybe never) made the first move to reconcile. And I knew it would be in the small battles on the couch where victory would be won. It felt really, really hard to swallow my pride and let go. But it also felt right.

I picked up the remote. I moved it to the ottoman and then slid over and gave Dave a hug. I whispered, "I care about you."

He hugged me back.

The new story is written in moments like this. These are defining moments, when we listen with God-intuition about how to live into the new story.

Hearing God: But When?

As in any relationship, *when* we communicate with God will vary. Ephesians 6:18 exhorts us to "pray in the Spirit on all occasions with all kinds of prayers and requests." First Thessalonians 5:17 tells us to "pray without ceasing" (ESV). There are times in the Gospels when Jesus intentionally went away to pray, and many other times when He clearly was in communion with His heavenly Father as He went about His work, receiving guidance and direction among the crowds. I believe we need a steady diet of both conversational and intentional communication with God. Our conversational communication will flow out of our intentional communication.

Conversational communication describes our quick check-ins throughout the day, similar to the couch moment I had with Dave. It is setting our hearts to always listen for what God desires in any situation. Conversational communication takes the form of a simple, deep-breath prayer like "Father in heaven, I trust You," a moment of praise between appointments or in the car, a call for help in a tricky situation or conversation, or a spirit of worship when walking outside or before bed.

Intentional communication is time set aside specifically to learn more about God's nature and to clarify our commitment to Him. We come to these times expecting to hear from God. Whether during a worship service, in a conversation with another believer, during time reading Scripture, or during time we've set aside to actively listen for God's direction, our role is to *believe* that God desires to speak to us in every situation. Because we can ask God to "give [us] life . . . according to [His] word" (Psalm 119:107, ESV), we should expect an infusion of life simply by being in His presence.

Worship and community with other believers become a priority. We expect God to speak to us, both individually and communally. We welcome His presence and tune our hearts to receive a message of truth and of life.

When it comes to your individual time with God, you may feel unsure of where to start or what to do. That's normal. A new relationship always takes some cultivating, especially at first. For generations, one spiritual practice Christians have used to open their minds to hear God's voice is *lectio divina*, which is Latin for "divine reading." Lectio divina has four components: reading, reflecting, praying, and contemplating. John of the Cross said, "Seek in reading and you will find in meditation; knock in prayer and it will be opened to you in contemplation."[6]

The practice consists of the following steps:

1. **Read** a selected Scripture passage slowly.
2. **Read** it again, listening for a word, phrase, or image that stands out to you, and looking for where you might find yourself in the passage. What character, metaphor, or object do you relate to?
3. **Reflect** after reading the passage for a third time. Consider why the words or images from step 2 stood out to you.
4. **Pray**, asking God, *What does this mean, and how does it connect to my life today?*
5. **Contemplate** by staying in that thought for a few moments. Wait on God, or simply rest in His presence. You may not receive immediate answers.

Not all conversations resolve in one short time with God. Most are running threads that may continue for weeks or months at a time.

There are many resources to help you grow in lectio divina. One of my favorites is a devotional called *The Message: Solo*, which uses *The Message* paraphrase of the Bible and provides some questions alongside each reading to help you with this practice.

You can get further practice in *The Struggle Is Real DVD Experience* and *Participant's Guide*, but I've included another opportunity below based on what we've learned together about hearing God. I'm praying for each one of you, that God would spark your imagination for Him, deepen your hunger for Him, and make Himself known personally and deeply to you today.

Keeping It Real

Before you move on from this chapter, I invite you to set aside fifteen to twenty minutes tonight or tomorrow morning to practice intentional communication with God. Don't expect fireworks and visions, but do expect to encounter God through His Word in an important way for your soul.

By intentionally opening your heart to God and His Word, you are writing new words into your story. You probably won't immediately connect your Struggle with every moment in the Word, but later in the day or later in the week, God will remind you of what you need to know. Remember that He promises, "You will seek me and find me when you seek me with all your heart" (Jeremiah 29:13).

I often begin my time with God with a few deep breaths and a short prayer: *Lord, I want to seek You with all my heart.* Today we will focus on Psalm 19.

1. **Read** the psalm slowly. If it will help you pay attention, read it out loud.

2. **Read** the psalm again, listening for a word, phrase, or image that stands out to you and seeing where you might find yourself in the passage. What character, metaphor, or object do you relate to?

3. **Reflect:** Read the passage for a third time. Reflect on why you think the words or images from your second reading stood out to you.

4. **Pray:** Ask God, *What does this mean and how does it connect to my life today?*

5. **Contemplate:** Stay in that thought for a few moments. Wait on God, or simply rest in His presence. Remember that you may not receive immediate answers. Not all conversations resolve in one short time with God. Most are running threads that might continue for weeks or months at a time.

8

The Beginnings
Know Your Roots

Parenting is a delicate balance of convincing
your kid they can do anything in life . . .
while also screaming "Don't do that!"
every three minutes.

UNKNOWN

Margaret Thatcher said, "You may have to fight a battle more than once to win it." Living into your new story won't happen overnight. If we let them, the broken parts in each of us will always exert some control over the choices we make. Victory in Christ often occurs in small loops, as we find ourselves circling back to old patterns and then slowly experiencing old bonds breaking as we push forward into new freedom and continually seek to hear God's voice.

Every time we get back on the freedom cycle, we can learn afresh how God is re-forming our hearts to our full glory in Him. So much of what we struggle with has winding and fibrous roots anchored deep in our broken stories.

If we want to become wise, we will have to go back in our histories before we can go forward. Remember the Good Life Inventory you completed in chapter 1? If you flip back to your answers, you may be reminded of the full and free life we are all looking for. In order to be people who don't experience the same repeated struggles, we often have to trace back in our story lines to find their sources—and to invite God's healing. The first of three story lines that we all have to reckon with is our own origins—our childhoods. We don't look back because we want to blame, justify, or vilify. We don't look back alone. We do it with Christ as the hero of our stories, and we do it so that we might pull up unhealthy roots and plant seeds of faith, peace, and hope. So we begin the replanting with a look back at where we began, where the old story was written. We look back as we seek to rewrite the new story, changing the way we view yesterday so we have freedom to be different today.

Beginnings: Family Matters

Let's do a one-word association. Are you ready? After you read the word below, write the very next word that comes to mind:

FAMILY—_____

If I could gather up everyone's responses, they would likely be as unique as our fingerprints. Some readers will think of words in the loving category, like *warm, affectionate, safe, loving,* or *kind.* Others will come up with words on the other side of that, like *broken, abusive, nonexistent, sham,* or *crazy.* Most will probably think of a word somewhere in between, and some people may struggle to pick just one word, because *family* floods us with all kinds of conflicting thoughts and feelings.

Family is complicated. But family is also where God most often reveals Himself. In the Ten Commandments (Exodus 20), we are instructed to honor our parents. A sign of faithful church leaders is their ability to manage their families (1 Timothy 3:1-5). Jesus calls people who believe in Him His sisters and brothers (Hebrews 2:11-12), and a special kind of love and care is reserved for the "family of believers" (1 Peter 2:17). Since God uses the family as a means of helping us understand life in Him, and since we all bring our own baggage to that word, then it's worth paying attention to what we know about our earthly families and how that impacts our struggles today and choices tomorrow. Here are a few reality checks to get us started:

Reality check #1: Dysfunction is the new normal... and the old normal.

Every family is a dysfunctional family. The only difference is the degree of imperfection. That means the family you grew up in, the one you might be raising now, even the one you've created with friends—all are flawed. We are broken-storied people who come together and do the best we can to love one another well—but we are still some shade of crazy.

I remember when I first told my mom our family was

dysfunctional. I was twenty-six years old, studying family systems in graduate school. I had just mapped out our genogram, a diagram that details a family for about three generations. Using symbols for shorthand, I detailed our family history—events like births and deaths, marriages and divorces, abuse and addiction. I also used lines to indicate the relational status between family members. A line that didn't fully join indicated a broken relationship. A jagged line signified an actively conflictual relationship. Dotted lines illustrated a distant one. By the time I'd finished drawing our family history, it looked like a preschooler had furiously scribbled all over the page. *Aha!* I thought to myself. *Finally someone understands what I've been insisting on for all five years of my adult life.*

I called my mom and detailed our dysfunction. I may have been a *shade* overdramatic, but it seemed like very important information that had to be revealed right then, even though my mother had been living in the crazy for the past fifty years. She entertained my urgent revelations, but then changed the subject. I remember thinking that she must not get it, because if she did, *everything would be different!* My sweet young self believed all our family needed was insight and everything would change. Every hurt would be undone; every misunderstanding would be made right. But as it turns out, making sweeping judgmental statements about how bad my childhood was (which I now realize sounded to my mom like I was declaring, "You are a terrible mother") was not the best way to handle this, *ahem*, revelation.

What my mother knew at fifty that I didn't have a clue

about in my twenties was that a diagram wasn't going to change dysfunction, and relationships within family aren't easy to boil down to symbols and lines. She'd been living in that complicated puzzle we called "family" a lot longer than I had. She knew that perhaps the most important thing we could do was try to understand *and* learn to live with it—and perhaps even love the broken-storied people within.

The good news is that family dysfunction is not new. If you want to feel better about your own upbringing, spend some time in the Old Testament. Adam's son Cain killed his brother, Abel. Noah got drunk and disgraced his family. Abraham slept with his wife's servant in order to have a child, defying God's promise that his wife would bear his son. Isaac played favorites with his twin boys, turning them against each other. Jacob's sons were so dysfunctional that they sold one brother into slavery and then led their dad to believe he'd been murdered. And that's just the first book of the Bible! Scripture doesn't tell stories that paint a perfect picture of family—it shows us realistic pictures and gives us a vision for a different future.

Reality check #2: Family is critical in your story.

It may go without saying, but the family in which you were raised largely drives the way you feel, think, and act today. The impact of your early life goes deep. Here's a list of just some of the areas of your well-being as an adult that are affected by the way your parents interacted with you as a child:

- Your ability to stand up for yourself
- Your ability to maintain friendships
- Your overall economic success
- Your engagement with work
- The health of your close relationships
- Your ability to handle emotions
- Your likelihood of depression[1]

Not only do your early experiences affect your current life choices, but your general attitude toward communication, conflict, discipline, money, sex, and family values are all deeply impacted by the family you grew up in.

Perhaps you read this list and think, *I'm doomed.* You know you were raised in particularly difficult circumstances, and you are well aware of the ways that's impacting you today, despite how hard you've tried to run away from that past. Or maybe you now realize that your family was actually a pretty great place to be raised, but you still struggle nonetheless, which makes you feel all the more guilty. It's easy to read this list and think of all the ways it crystalizes your success or failure. But the point of examining this list is not to make a bleak prediction on your future. It's to help you better understand the world you grew up in so that you can make wise choices for the life you are creating as an adult. So often, we struggle against invisible forces that we have not looked at or named. We only see the struggle; we don't see its source.

A family is a complex system, with each "actor" in that system playing a role. In other words, it's not just your family that matters—it's what you brought to that family, the temperament you were born with.

Reality check #3: Your personality matters in the story.

When my two oldest kids were preschoolers, I learned an important lesson on how temperament affects the way people engage with and experience family life. Charlie, my oldest, is conscientious and deliberate. He is a rule follower who will always look before he leaps—and may decide that the leap isn't worth it after all. Cameron, my daughter, while also conscientious, is more likely to exert her own opinion, often leaping before looking. This metaphor proved itself true—literally—one summer at the pool.

At the time, I was hugely pregnant with our third child. That summer was so hot and humid that everyone began sweating as soon as they hit the outside air. As you can imagine, I was a special kind of cranky reserved for pregnant moms with two toddlers. Since my biggest concern when parenting young children was keeping them alive, I found myself raising my voice to keep a young and enthusiastic Cameron from following her brother wherever he went—particularly off the side of the pool. Whenever Charlie jumped, Cameron wanted to follow suit. In fact, she kept leaping into the pool before I could get my swollen belly in position to receive her little spider-monkey legs flying at me.

Mr. Tentative would wait for a moment before leaping, while I encouraged, "Go ahead, buddy! Come on, jump!" Charlie would still be midair as I warned little Cameron behind him, *"Not yet, Cameron! Don't go!"* Charlie would hesitate again; Cameron would need a louder warning to stop. This became a pattern. One child needed encouragement; the other needed a warning, and I usually needed to give both in the same breath.

"*Charlie, you go! C'mon, Charlie, go! No, wait—not you, Cameron! You stop! Stop!*" As if I didn't seem crazy before, now I was giving completely opposite directions at the top of my breath, occasionally throwing the dog's name in there too, shouting commands wildly in all directions.

After a few months of this, I began to notice a pattern. Whenever I changed my voice to take on a "Mama Bear" tone to keep Cameron from some potential death trap, Charlie would cower. I could see him shrink back a bit and lower his eyes, a look of concern washing over his face. I would pull Cameron back from whatever edge of doom she was teetering on and then turn to him: "Honey, I wasn't talking to you. I was telling Cameron to stop." Once he started to cry and told me, "Mom, you are always *yelling* at me . . ." Friends, I promise you I wasn't yelling that particular time. (I do yell often. But not then.) Yet I realized that the conscientious, sensitive child received my change of tone as yelling. The free-spirited, stronger-willed child couldn't even hear me talking until I used that sharper tone of voice. All three of us were experiencing the exact same moment, but experiencing it completely differently because of our temperaments.[2]

Remember our "old story" formula?

Who We Are + Moments That Matter = Stories We Live

Your temperament is a huge part of who you are. This means that the way you experienced your family is hugely important to the way you understand life today. You may have been raised by great parents in a loving home, but maybe you were particularly sensitive to conflict. If so, even healthy conflict may leave you feeling unstable and frightened. You may have been a strong-willed child raised by a sensitive mother—and her insecurity about how to parent you has led to your own insecurity about your strength of personality today. Because of your temperament, your memories of your family experience may be vastly different from what your siblings or parents recall. Understanding what you bring to your family system helps shape your understanding of the particular joys and struggles you remember—and understanding your own temperament impacts the way you move forward with relationships today.

If you've never explored your personality, I encourage you to do so. You can find many free temperament inventories online.[3] One of the best things about taking a personality inventory is that it can put words or phrases to long-held feelings or experiences that you didn't know how to express. These inventories are not a crystal ball that reveal your future; they are just a springboard for meaningful reflection on how you perceive the world and how that impacts your engagement with your story and with God. Finding language to describe these parts of you can be incredibly helpful as you understand your old story and your new story in Christ. It can also help others engage with your story in new and meaningful ways. (For a fuller discussion of temperament and how it impacts your story, see *The Struggle Is Real Participant's Guide*.)

Reality check #4: Dysfunction is contagious.

Not only do your temperament and family experiences affect how you understand your role in your life story, you are also deeply impacted by those around you. When you are around unhealthy people, you are far more likely to respond in unhealthy ways. In other words, *crazy makes crazy*. Conversely, when you are around healthy and generally happy people, you are far more likely to be happy yourself. This concept is known as emotional contagion, but long before any psychologists studied it, God made this idea clear in Scripture. Proverbs 13:20 says, "Walk with the wise and become wise, for a companion of fools suffers harm."

I once talked with a woman—let's call her Debbie—who was considering leaving her husband. He had been unfaithful, and although he had confessed one incident to her, Debbie had recently discovered texts and e-mails that convinced her he was still involved with another woman. She was torn because of her love for him, but she was also enraged by his actions. The next time we met, she told me, quite casually, that she had gotten involved with another man. Her husband was upset when he found out, and she was indignant. She leaned toward me, her face red. "How could he be upset with *me* after what he's done?"

Believe me, friends, there is nothing as excruciating as the kind of betrayal Debbie endured. However, when she chose her revenge in the arms of another man, the pain in their relationship multiplied. She answered his dysfunction with more dysfunction, which only made the pit deeper.

I share this example because many of us fall into the victim/villain mentality—that one person is always in the wrong and the other is always in the right—but life is a whole lot more complicated than that. Debbie's husband was 100 percent wrong when he betrayed their marriage vows, but Debbie's response was also wrong. And as hard as it is to face, we must see that our actions are our own responsibility. Romans 14:12 says, "Yes, each of us will give a personal account to God" (NLT). The actions of others don't factor into the *personal* account we must give. Only our own actions are relevant, but we must be aware of how the people in our stories affect our way of living. This doesn't mean we need to ditch anyone who isn't perfectly healthy and happy—of course, none of us could meet that standard! It *does* mean that we need to consider how our relationships impact our ability to be healthy. Debbie and her husband were living in a dysfunctional pattern of relationship long before the first affair. And dysfunction always breeds dysfunction, with roots that extend deep into our stories.

Because we are all dysfunctional on some level, we are impacted by one another's dysfunction. As children, we all needed a perfect mom and dad—and not one of us had a perfect mom or dad (or for that matter, can *be* a perfect mom or dad!). We are all influenced by one another's sin, in major and minor ways. We all emit emotions that other people "catch."

If you were surrounded by positivity growing up, you

are far more likely to be positive. If a depressed parent raised you, you are more prone to depression. This is true whether or not your parents were Christians. *We are all dysfunctional.* The struggle is real because the struggle is sin, and the four-way broken relationships impact each and every one of us.

But the hope of our stories is the truth we began with: The struggle is real, but the struggle is also *good.* The good comes when we make God the main character in our stories; when we follow today's dysfunction back into the old story and let it reveal deeper truth. The good comes in recognizing those deep places of brokenness within us and bringing them to God. The good comes when we ask God to reveal the source of our broken places and then to bring us healing and health so we can live differently tomorrow. The incredible reality of Jesus Christ is in His ability to move freely through all chapters of your story. That means that although you might be living in chapter 9, Jesus can be back in chapter 2, showing up unexpectedly in my perm story and Debbie's marriage story and the place in your story where you feel stuck and hurt, the place that is still trying to define your future.

There's Always a Pattern

Now I invite you to consider a pattern of struggle in your life and look at its origins. Perhaps a person comes to mind. What about this individual is hard for you? What makes it harder to deal with this particular person than, say, your best friend? Usually, there is some lethal combination that's being created between the two of you. Maybe it's her insecurity and your anger. Maybe it's his control and your fear of dependency. Maybe it's a previous conflict that isn't resolved because you both are conflict avoidant. For the most part, ongoing struggles with other people are related to some fear or insecurity that we've both experienced before.

When it comes to recognizing how your growing-up family impacts your choices today, remember that *there's always a sin pattern behind our inner battles.* This simply means that there are patterns in your family that, if left unchecked, you will repeat. When we hear the term *sin pattern,* we usually think of big and dramatic sin, like infidelity or addiction or abuse. But the truth is that subtle sin patterns play out in our lives all the time. Take a look at the following short list of sin patterns that often occur in families:

Potential Dysfunctional (Sin) Patterns
- Dysfunctional conflict (conflict avoidance, passive-aggressive behavior, physical or emotional abuse)
- Lying (keeping up appearances, maintaining a certain "image")
- Scapegoating (blaming others for every struggle, victim mentality)
- Betrayal/hypocrisy (differences between our public and private lives)
- Health issues (lack of self-care, fear of illness/loss, etc.)
- Unhealthy relationship to food, technology, or alcohol

- Issues with sexuality (infidelity, gender roles, overly fearful/legalistic environment, or overly sexual/permissive environment)
- Lack of forgiveness (inability/unwillingness between family members to offer sincere apologies)
- Love of money (greed, hoarding, fear, materialism)
- Achievement fixation (worth and identity attached to education, accolades, "winning")

Whew! If you are like me (and every graduate psychology student ever), you've realized that, heck yeah, your family is dysfunctional. Maybe you identify with at least one problem in every area on the list! But this isn't about deciding who has the worst family. This is about acknowledging the subtle but powerful ways we've been shaped by the sin patterns of our own families. Truth has power, but only when it's used to impact the choices we make for tomorrow. Recognizing a pattern doesn't excuse our own behavior, but it can provide the motivation and insight we need to address areas of temptation and weakness in our own lives and to understand the way our past experiences often inform our future choices.

I have a friend who grew up with a mother who prioritized "keeping up appearances" above honesty. When my friend was a senior in high school, she got an older friend to buy liquor for her and her friends before Homecoming. My friend left the pre-party just before the drinking was discovered. Her buddies were caught and suspended from school. My friend's conscience was tormented by the fact that not only had she been drinking, but she had been the one who arranged to get alcohol for her friends.

My friend couldn't stand hiding, so she told her mother the whole story. She wanted to confess to her school administrators and accept her punishment. Her mother was livid with her *for wanting to be honest.* Mom was concerned that her daughter could ruin her chances to be accepted into a prestigious college because of the potential black mark on her record. She forbade my friend from telling the school. My friend was trapped. Should she honor her conviction and betray her mother, or should she betray her conscience and obey her mother?

Here's the craziest part. I heard this story more than twenty years after it happened. Decades later, my friend was still tormented by this incident. As a teenager, she had unwittingly been trapped in her family's own sin pattern. And as an adult, she is a self-admitted people pleaser who struggles to stand up for herself.

Working though family dysfunction, whether major or minor, takes rigorous effort. It takes a commitment to God's healing. It takes the company of healthy friends or mentors who will listen to your experience and help you find God's hand in it. For my friend, the healing began when she first told the story—twenty years after the fact. The healing continued when she decided that even though it felt like a silly story now, she needed to deal with it once and for all. The fear monster that kept her from telling the truth began to shrink as she spoke about the memory. She overcame her incessant need to please others only when she realized she'd been trapped in her mother's sin pattern of fear and insecurity. Although she couldn't change her mother, my friend determined not to remain stuck in that pattern herself.

My friend can stand up for herself now and see her conscience not as a liability but as a gift to the world. As she traced her current struggles back to that Homecoming, she recognized that experience as a crucial chapter in her life of faith. It caused a crisis of conscience that prepared her for what was next. Just a year after that incident, she was introduced to a relationship with Christ. She now looks back at her dilemma over whether to follow her conscience or her mom's order and sees it as a time when the Holy Spirit was moving and helping her recognize her own need for redemption. The struggle was very real, and that struggle was very good—it led her to acknowledge her brokenness to Christ for the first time. But just because she became a Christian doesn't mean she immediately began living in the new story. Only twenty years later was she finally able to break free of all its ramifications in her teenage life.

Each of us inherits sin patterns we will have to overcome. It may be image-oriented living or approval-seeking decision making. It may be a pattern of greed or ambition or fear. It may be different for you than for your siblings; it may be a new pattern you recognize as you continue to live the chapters of your own story. But every time we call out these patterns, every time we forgive those who intentionally or unintentionally hurt us with their own sin, we are active agents in our new stories. We are letting go of the old story and making room for the new.

Perhaps you are realizing for the first time how unhealthy your relationships have been. Maybe you now realize you are duplicating the very patterns in your family you vowed never to repeat. Maybe you are like Debbie, taking out your hurt on other people, repeating a cycle of dysfunction and pain that threatens to ruin the life you've built.

Without Jesus' power to make things new and to bring hope to even the hardest experiences, we truly are captive to our temperaments and families of origin. We are not made new; we are simply recycled products of our parents and grandparents, whether for good or for evil. Four times in the Old Testament, we read: "Yet he [God] does not leave the guilty unpunished; he punishes the children and their children for the sin of the parents to the third and fourth generation."[4]

God is not cursing innocent children because of their parents' behavior. He is pointing out the reaping-and-sowing mentality. We will reap the dysfunction of our parents and our parents' parents unless there is an intervention. We will absolutely live the old story unless there is a rescue. The genograms of every family speak of this reality—we will reap what those before us have sown. If they've sown dysfunction and brokenness, we will reap that sin.

This is reflected by every woman who's ever shocked herself and said, "Oh my gosh, I sound just like my mother!" Every man who's found himself repeating the same actions of his father understands this reality too.

We have the same effect on future generations. Those around us—our children and other people we influence—will reap what we've sown. It's not a condemnation; it's a law of nature.

This is where the beautiful good news of Christ enters into our stories. Remember the actor/agent/author study, which said that the healthiest people have a "redemption story"? Redemption is such a huge part of the whole story of life because God is the greatest Redeemer of all time. To redeem means to "gain or regain possession of (something) in exchange for payment."[5] Here's another definition:

Redeem:
to free from what **distresses** or harms: as
a: to **free from captivity** by payment of ransom
b: to **extricate** from or help to overcome something detrimental
c: to **release** from blame or debt: clear
d: to **free from the consequences** of sin[6]

By virtue of this definition, there cannot be redemption without struggle, whether distress, harm, captivity, blame, or consequences. The struggle comes from the law of nature that leads us to reap from the sin nature of our parents and our parents' parents unless Christ intervenes. And it's in the struggle that we find the intervention. The intervention is always the love of Christ, which interrupts our stories with the promise of redemption.

When Jesus explained the work of His death and resurrection to His disciples, He poured wine into a cup and said, "This cup is the new covenant in my blood, which is poured out for you" (Luke 22:20). Ephesians 1:7 says we have redemption through Christ's blood. When we take Communion, when we come to the table Jesus set for us—when we eat the bread and drink the wine—we are saying that we accept our new bloodline. The dysfunction that is in "our blood"—passed down by our families—is no longer our dysfunction. Something new is in our blood. It's the blood of Christ, pulsing through us with new and eternal life, slowly inviting us into a new story.

When Debbie came to my office for counsel, I think she was looking for my approval of her divorce. What neither of us expected was that Debbie would accept her own part in the dysfunction. As she acknowledged the truth about the relationship she had pursued, her heart softened toward her husband. It did not make his choices *right*. It did not dismiss the pain. But it did allow Debbie to own her dysfunction; to trace her own story back to her relationship with her dad (who had an affair when Debbie was a teenager). It allowed Debbie to seek counseling and to establish new boundaries within her marriage. I don't know what the long-term status of her marriage will be. I don't know if both Debbie and her husband can break out of their own hurt and overcome the enormous struggles within their marriage. But I do know that it takes only one person to change a system. I do know that dysfunction is contagious, but the more we are aware of it, the less likely we are to fall prey to its whims. I do know that God is the great Redeemer who can rebuild a life out of any ashes, no matter how destructive the fire has been. I do know that we can enter into a new bloodline when we receive the life of Christ.

Though no one escapes the struggle, we all have a choice to make about how the struggle writes the story. God offers us a way to move forward through our struggles in three ways: by providing a new definition of family, a new perspective on hardship, and the wisdom to move forward in healthy ways.

A New Family

In Christ, we have been given a new family. Our family of origin is no longer our primary source of relationship and love, although it is still important to continue honoring them (more on that later). Many people react to family dysfunction by pushing relatives away and becoming an island of independence—thinking this will give them the freedom they crave. Over time, however, estranging ourselves from family members without seeking healing and forgiveness is as damaging as not leaving our families at all. It is a reaction to the hurt caused by our families, not a healthy way to live. We were made for interdependence, yet when God redeems us, our primary source of dependence moves to Him.

Jesus modeled this on earth by honoring His mother, Mary, even as His unrelenting priority was His heavenly Father's work. When His family requested that He stop teaching and come out to meet them, Jesus told them, "My mother and brothers are those who hear God's word and put it into practice" (Luke 8:21). This is such a clarifying truth: God's way and will must come above all else, even our own mothers and fathers.

Of course, Scripture also makes clear that we are called

to honor our families. The Ten Commandments, Proverbs, and the teaching of Jesus and Paul speak of honoring parents with our words and deeds, as well as taking care of our families' physical needs.[7] Yet the Bible also reminds us that God is greatest, and following His way of life is our first priority. In families with particularly challenging and even abusive relationships, the way we honor our families must be balanced with our personal pursuit of health and wholeness, and requires wise counsel from our godly friends and leaders who can help us strike the balance in if—and how—we maintain relationships.

Philosopher Jean-Paul Sartre said, "Freedom is what you do with what's been done to you." We can be set free from the sin patterns that have defined our lives, but we are responsible to do something with that freedom and to be changed by it. In Christ, we are given "the right to become children of God . . . born of God" (John 1:12-13). In Christ, the needs our families didn't meet can become places of growth where we look to God to meet those needs through communion with Him and community with others.

When speaking of generational sin patterns, the preacher Charles Spurgeon said, "The Holy Spirit can come and remove from you the taint of heredity so that you shall be able to overcome this special tendency of yours—and you shall be preserved from those sins which run in your blood, which are in your constitution through your birth. God can help you! He that made the watch can mend it. He that made you, can set you right, again!"[8]

As a member of God's family, the pressure is off your family.

Being known, secure, and loved in your eternal family allows you to engage with your earthly family in a different way.

A New Perspective

As I was writing this section, two friends unexpectedly dropped by for a visit. As I often do, I turned them into a two-person focus group and asked them this question: "How does knowing Christ change your perspective on life's hardships?"

My friend Ellie answered first. She said, "I know this might sound simple, but as I've experienced God as the source of love, I no longer bring that same level of need to the relationships I'm in. When I find myself looking for affirmation at work, I can remind myself that all of my needs have already been met in God's love for me. I guess it's just like a victory mind-set. All the hard work has already been done. It totally changes the way I engage with my own needs from insecurities and wounds."

Drew thought for another moment and then said, "If I'm in a rough patch or whatever, I know it's just a season. I can always have hope for a new day. I know it's temporary, and I can place temporary value on it. I can't imagine trying to have temporary things—good or bad—try to meet my eternal needs. God completely changes my perspective."

One of the magnificent things about Christ's work in our stories is His ability to redeem and transfigure places of hardship or wounding. Because of this, we always have hope that things can be different and our own perspective can change. Scripture tells us that it's in the midst of our hardships that we will experience this shift. The apostle Paul says we can rejoice when we run into problems because "they help us develop endurance. And endurance develops strength of character, and character strengthens our confident hope of salvation" (Romans 5:3-4, NLT). That's what Drew was talking about when he spoke of finding the hope in the eternal rather than the temporary. Even in a "rough patch," we have a different perspective because we know this isn't the end. The passage from Romans goes on to speak of this particular kind of hope, which will never lead to disappointment. It is unshakable because it's rooted in the unchanging, faithful, and absolute love and truth of God. "For we know how dearly God loves us, because he has given us the Holy Spirit to fill our hearts with his love. When we were utterly helpless, Christ came at just the right time and died for us sinners" (verses 5-6, NLT).

Out of our struggles comes this new perspective: Difficulties lead to character that leads to hope that brings us right back to the new story. While we were helpless, Christ became the redeeming hero of our stories. As a result, the Holy Spirit now fills us with love.

A New Vision of Health

God also gives us a way through our struggles with a new vision for what health means. Proverbs 24:14 says, "Know also that wisdom is like honey for you: If you find it, there is a future hope for you, and your hope will not be cut off." God's love is restorative and powerful. His renewing love strengthens us inwardly day by day (2 Corinthians 4:16). That means that every time we embrace the truth that *God is greatest, and He knows best,* we can become healthier. The Good Life Inventory from chapter 1 is based on what wise living actually looks like as described in Scripture. Here's how the Amplified version of James 3:17 describes such wisdom:

> The wisdom from above is first pure [morally and spiritually undefiled], then peace-loving [courteous, considerate], gentle, reasonable [and willing to listen], full of compassion and good fruits. It is unwavering, without [self-righteous] hypocrisy [and self-serving guile].

Imagine being described like this every day: "[Insert your name here] _____ has an intact moral compass and is courteous and considerate of others, gentle and reasonable in decisions, full of compassion, unwavering and resolute, transparent and authentic." That's a person I want to be friends with. That's a person I want to follow. That's a person I want to *be.* This is the promise of walking in wisdom.

Many years after my call to my mom during graduate school, she laughs when we call the family dysfunctional. That's what the Struggle can do. When we let our stories be redefined by the new story, we find ourselves coloring in the old lines with grace. Grace lets people be broken and doesn't put the pressure that only Christ can handle on them. Grace lets us stand up for ourselves without fearing our identities will be crushed if we don't receive our loved ones' approval.

Grace allows us to draw boundary lines that are healthy and limit access to the vulnerable parts of ourselves with unhealthy people. Grace gives us choices.

When we let our stories be redefined by the new story, we find ourselves coloring in the old lines with grace.

You see, not only is dysfunction contagious—but health is too. It takes only one person to change an entire family system. It takes only one person on the freedom cycle to affect everyone else. This change won't be like transformation TV. It won't happen overnight, and it won't happen without a struggle. There will be inevitable setbacks. (Who among us hasn't turned back into a surly teenager when invited home for Thanksgiving?) But the truth remains that emotional health is contagious. When we pursue health in our lives—when we pursue healthy people—we move toward health. When we make our heavenly Father our only perfect parent, we are able to forgive our flawed earthly parents. When we make Christ the hero of our stories, He transfigures them—every bit of them—into something new. The struggles remain. But we become different.

Keeping It Real

1. What are two to three aspects of your family system that you'd like to continue? What are two to three sin patterns you'd like to break?

2. Do you recognize patterns in your current life that are a reflection of the old story? Where do you need God's intervention in your life?

3. Consider the Jean-Paul Sartre quote: "Freedom is what you do with what's been done to you." In what ways do you need to act on the freedom you have in Christ?

The New Language
Rewrite Your Thoughts

Words make worlds.

KRISTA TIPPETT

I want to tell you something true about living into your new story: It's going to be a little scary.

When Jesus interrupts your existence with something as extraordinary as a rewrite of your identity, it's more than a little disconcerting. When Jesus uses the word *life*—as in "whoever finds their life will lose it" (Matthew 10:39), He isn't being superficial in His description of what you are giving up. The rewrite of your story in Christ will permeate every part of your identity and every relationship—with God, yourself, others, and the world. To give your life over for His life means you give up control of how those relationships go.

When I first told the perm story to that gaggle of middle school girls, something cracked in me that couldn't be repaired. What felt like a painful breaking was actually the beginning of the new story, a story I've been living into ever since. Control of my life shifted hands when I wasn't even looking, and all of a sudden, relationships began changing. I hungered for God in a different way, and I found myself reading Scripture with the sense that it really mattered, seeking answers, comfort, and encouragement. The Bible started feeling real. I would read stories and there would be words that would lift off the page, speaking directly into this *unlike-me* with whom I was becoming acquainted. My inner world started spilling out when I wasn't expecting it. I began crying during church, completely unprovoked and without real "angst"—just tears, flowing every single time I entered a worship service. It was so *unlike me*, at least the me I was familiar with, the me I was comfortable with, the me that didn't surprise with tears and longings and spiritual experiences.

One day I was on the phone with my friend Pete, and I hesitatingly began to tell him about this uncomfortable new reality. I explained that I was *feeling* things, as if every emotional wire in my soul had been stripped of its protective coating and was buzzing and sparking, ready to burn down the whole old story I'd been living. Everything was impacted: my belief that there was a new and different story for me, my desire to live wholeheartedly, and my awareness of the effects of growing up in my family.

My angst wasn't because I didn't want to live in my new story; it was because I didn't really know what the new story was, and that felt dangerous. I was excited and worried all at once. Excited because I was beginning to believe in the enormous reality of the Kingdom of God here on earth—a Kingdom I was experiencing in my own heart. But I was worried, too, about many things—mostly how other people might react. I asked Pete, "But what about my husband? What about my friends? This isn't the Nicole they know. This isn't the Nicole they committed to. What if I change and they don't? *Is this normal?*" The "this" I was referring to was the new language of life—a story where God is real, He interacts with people like me, and He asks us to leave our old lives to come into His Kingdom, *and really means it.* The "this" was the fact that I was actually believing that Jesus is real, that God speaks, and that we can become a "new creation." I was experiencing what the Bible calls being "born again," and I had no idea what this experience meant for everyone else in my story.

Yes, a life rewrite is scary. Perhaps you can relate. Most of the time when change comes to our lives, we immediately begin to experience the tension of the old story even while we feel the hope and freedom of the new. Moving from the old story to the new may happen like this for you, or it may glide in slowly like a sunrise. Most likely, it'll happen in a myriad of ways, one defining moment at a time. And because words are the primary way we shape our stories, your new story will be shaped by new words—new words for God, for yourself, for your relationships, and for the world.

The Gospel of John begins like this: "In the beginning was the Word, and the Word was with God, and the Word was

God." Why is Jesus called the Word? Perhaps it is because, as author Krista Tippett says, "words make worlds."[1] Our lives are shaped by the words we read, hear, and speak. Our lives are shaped by the words we've known as truth, whether the internal agreements we made early in life about ourselves, the words that have been spoken to us or about us, or the words that have become the defining feature of our lives. Some words carry deep emotional currents: *Mother. Father. Best friend. Boyfriend. Wife.*

Sometimes a mere word or phrase spoken to us about who we could be becomes a defining moment in our lives. Recall from chapter 3 how Abigail called out David's true identity when she said, "You fight the LORD's battles" (1 Samuel 25:28), an invitation into the better story of his life that convinced him to trust God.

Words can also be wielded like weapons. A demeaning label spoken in anger can be a violent assault against the essence of us. Some words carry condemnation and shame, heavy like an iron apron of judgment over our hearts: *Useless. Lazy. Stupid. Idiot.* When words are used as ammunition, we become confused and disoriented about the truth of who we are. Those piercing words, even when unwelcome, form our inner perception of ourselves. We can trace the shape of them, the tone of the voice that delivered them, or the curve of the handwriting that spelled them out. We can travel back to the very moment when those word-weapons were launched, when the assault broke something within us that has remained in ruins. A good friend of mine recalls with great clarity the moment in high school when one of his mentors told him, "You just aren't a leader." A decade later, my friend (who is in leadership) is still hounded by that simple phrase.

Words are potent, but there is a force even more powerful than our words. All words are trumped by *the* Word, the name given to Jesus in the beginning of John's Gospel, the capital-*w* Word—the defining Word in the world. When we put our trust in Christ, He becomes the defining Word in our lives.

My phone conversation with Pete was a decisive moment for me as I entered my new story. When I look back on it, I realize I was really asking Pete to give me words for a new story. He paused, and then as he always does, he gently pointed me to the Word. He reminded me of the story of Jesus' disciple Peter, a man on the brink of living from his new story, asking Jesus about His plans for the other disciples. And rather than lay out their stories, Jesus told Peter, "You must follow me" (John 21:22).

Pete took another pause, as he's prone to do when he's listening for God's direction, and then said gently, "Nicole, you follow Him. He'll work out the rest." Pete used a story to point me to my new story. The right stories will nurture us and guide us, allowing us to grow up into something new.

The Word on Words

Words are the way we transform invisible thoughts into external reality. This analogy carries through to our experience with Jesus. He is the Word who brings the invisible and inner reality of God into outward expression. Words, then, become part of the way we define ourselves and our reality.

Words are associated with wise living in Scripture. "The tongue has the power of life and death" within it, "presumably because it has the power to shape beliefs and convictions that affect eternal destinies."[2] Jesus connected our hearts to our words when He said, "Out of the abundance of the heart the mouth speaks" (Matthew 12:34, ESV). Our words flow both ways—out of the heart as our words are formed, and into our hearts as words are received. Said another way, when we let God shape us, we promise to "transfer to [our] lips all the counsel that comes from your mouth" (Psalm 119:13, MSG).

Psychologists theorize that children are born with an innate ability to learn the complexities of language at a rapid rate. Anyone who's been around toddlers recognizes their extraordinary capacity to pick up and retain words, even down to the emphasis and accent they use when repeating phrases they've heard. As a joke, we once told our young son to respond to the question "Are you ready?" with the answer "I was born ready!" For months afterward, Desmond would repeat "*I was born reeaaddy!*" with gusto, repeating the words with the same exact cadence and emphasis as the first time he'd heard it.

Not only are we innately wired for language and adept at picking up language from our environment, but we also think in words. Neurologist and psychologist Oliver Sacks noted:

> "We are our language," it is often said; but our real language, our real identity, lies in inner speech, in that ceaseless stream and generation of meaning that

constitutes the individual mind. It is through inner speech that the child develops his own concepts and meanings; it is through inner speech that he achieves his own identity; it is through inner speech, finally, that he constructs his own world.[3]

Our inner speech shapes our inner world, impacting our attitudes, behaviors, and engagement with the world outside of our heads. In our history, we've accumulated corners and closets and whole rooms in our souls that have been deeply impacted by this inner speech. If those rooms in your heart had names, what would you name them? Most all of us have a room of some size called Fear, where our inner speech is guarded and suspicious and perhaps even paranoid about the actions and intentions of those around us. Many of us are also familiar with rooms of Insecurity or Pride or Anger. When we find ourselves in circumstances that remind us of hurtful memories, we may find our speech influenced by our desire to protect ourselves from the next hard situation.

But to be transfigured in the new story is to revisit any rooms where our inner speech hasn't yet been touched by the transforming power of God's love. To be changed from the inside out requires new words. Let's examine how God's Word enables us to rewrite our internal scripts.

Rewriting Our Relationship with God

Most of us need to do significant rewriting of our inner scripts when it comes to understanding our heavenly Father. *Father* is a loaded word. Some of us have had incredible experiences with our fathers, but they are still human and flawed. Many of us had "bad dad" experiences. They weren't who we needed them to be, whether by intentional choice or unintentional circumstances. As children, we needed fathers who balanced the power of their protective abilities with the tenderness of their love. Some fathers exhibited power without tenderness. Others were tender but lacked strength. Only our heavenly Father is perfect in both power and love for His children. Yet without intentional effort, we will likely lean toward understanding God's power while discounting His affection or grasping His affection while underestimating His power.

God has given us His own words to describe the balance of power and love He offers to each one of us. He uses words like *lavish*, *delight*, and *affection* to describe how He feels about us. His power is evident in His work in the world, but perhaps His tender mercies aren't as close to your experience. I wonder what the voice of God sounds like to you when you think about it. Close your eyes and imagine hearing from God. What is the *tone* of His voice? Is it tinged in delight and affection or in condemnation and shame? Is it a voice of love or a voice of disapproval? Does God seem interested in you or bored by you?

To rewrite your story, you must first believe that *God is for you*. You must have an accurate understanding of His great, fierce, crazy, unrelenting love for you. When your inner voice sounds like anything but love, visualize yourself waving a red flag and then rewrite the script.

Remember, we've committed to the Bible being our

ultimate reality, and it repeatedly tells us who we are in Christ. Below are a few short verses you can memorize, recite, or pray through as you rewrite what it means to be loved by your heavenly Father. These are verses you can build a relationship on. These are verses that can become personal prayers. If you don't know God in this way, He longs to reveal Himself to you for who He really is. You can seek Him with these words and rewrite the script. Bring these truths close to your heart. Speak them aloud before you go to bed and when you wake up. Write them on your heart; cover the doors of the rooms of Fear and Insecurity and Disapproval with them.

Ten verses on who God actually is

The LORD set his affection on your ancestors and loved them.

DEUTERONOMY 10:15

The eyes of the LORD search the whole earth in order to strengthen those whose hearts are fully committed to him.

2 CHRONICLES 16:9, NLT

Our God, the great God, mighty and awesome, . . . keeps his covenant of love.

NEHEMIAH 9:32

Your love is better than life.

PSALM 63:3

Answer me, LORD, out of the goodness of your love;
in your great mercy turn to me.

PSALM 69:16

The LORD takes delight in his people; he crowns the
humble with victory.

PSALM 149:4

Because of the LORD's great love we are not consumed,
for his compassions never fail.

LAMENTATIONS 3:22

You . . . delight to show mercy.

MICAH 7:18

There is now no condemnation for those who are in
Christ Jesus.

ROMANS 8:1

See what great love the Father has lavished on us,
that we should be called children of God!

1 JOHN 3:1

Rewriting Our Relationship with Ourselves

We cannot separate God's love for us from our relationship
with ourselves—one will always impact the other.

I was once teaching the concept of Sabbath rest to a group
of women in a midweek Bible study. We had covered this

topic before, so I sought God in prayer as I end⟋ find a way to make the reality of resting in God ⌐⌐ own heart and relevant for each one of them. The Sunᴏᴀ⟍ morning before I taught, I was lying in bed preparing to begin the day. My mind was full of everything I needed to do to prepare for the upcoming week—set the car-pool schedule, come up with dinner menus, and buy my nephew's birthday gift, which would now be sent embarrassingly late. Out of that whirling dervish of thoughts came a still, small voice, a voice I've come to recognize as the Spirit's: *Why don't you take a Sabbath rest from feeling bad?* It was such a strange thought, so outside of my own rapid-fire planning mind-set, that I was taken aback.

Why don't you take a rest from feeling bad?

I recognize the voice of God because His tone is different from every other voice in my inner world. In this instance, His voice had a lightness to it, almost as if He had a chuckle caught in the back of His throat. The still, small voice I know delivers simple messages with joy and a tone of love.

Why don't you take a rest from feeling bad?

Well, okay, God, I guess I can do that.

So I did. I didn't think I felt that bad about myself, so I assumed this would be easy. I got up and went about my day, and every time a thought came to me about the way I was disappointing someone or doing something wrong or not well enough, I refused to dwell on it. When I told myself I wasn't pretty enough or energetic enough or fun enough or not *anything enough*, I reminded myself that I was taking a Sabbath rest from feeling bad. When I decided to take a nap that day, I didn't let myself think about the other things I should be doing. When I didn't make the greatest dinner, I didn't let myself think about how I was not meeting the full nutritional needs of my children. When I sat down in the middle of the afternoon and watched TV, I didn't let myself look down on myself for actually doing nothing. This happened dozens of times that day. *Dozens.* My inner critic, I discovered, was strong, demanding, and relentless.

As we begin to understand who God is, His love for us begins to change the way we feel about ourselves. As our relationship with God grows, our communication with Him flourishes, and He begins to change the way we treat ourselves. It's hard to be so harsh with ourselves when our heavenly Father is busy delighting in us.

I stood up the following Thursday morning and told this story to a few hundred women gathered in that room. When I explained how God had asked me to take a rest from feeling bad, I saw tears spring into eyes all around the room. The following week, I received e-mails and texts from women who had never given themselves permission to stop feeling bad about all the ways they were not enough. The very thought that the God of the universe would treat us with such tender kindness and *invite us to treat ourselves in the same way* is a powerful indicator of how deeply we need our stories to be rewritten. When we begin to understand God's essence and His heart toward us, the firstfruits of that relationship manifest in a new gentleness toward our own humanness, our frailty. When we humble ourselves to receive Him for who He really is, we can rewrite the script of our own inner speech.

Galatians 5:22-23 says that the fruit of the Spirit in us is love, joy, peace, patience, kindness, goodness, faithfulness, gentleness, and self-control. So often we talk about this fruit manifesting itself in our relationships with others, but I wonder if the first place that fruit appears is in our relationship with ourselves. Does your inner speech reflect an internal critic who's watching every move you make and analyzing every word that comes from your mouth, or does it speak in a voice that is loving, joyful, peaceful, kind? Is your inner voice patient with you, good to you, faithful to you, gentle in words and action? Most of us have a lot of rewriting to do in this area. I don't quite know why we are so harsh with ourselves. I'm not sure what's at work in us that is so demeaning and demanding, so critical and condemning. But I do know that it's not God. I believe it's a remnant of our broken selves, the inner voices that wrestle for control of our words and actions, the voices that try to use fear as a motivator and shame as a punishment.

Psychologist Ethan Kross led an experiment on how people can influence their inner critics. He found that one simple shift—referring to themselves in the third person ("him" or "her") and using their names rather than the pronoun *I*—led people to be kinder to themselves. People using this technique came across as "more rational, and less emotional" in their inner speech.[4] Imagine taking the ten promises of God previously mentioned and making them personal by inserting your own name.

> See what great love the Father has lavished on _____,
> that _____ is called a child of God!

> The Lord takes delight in _____; he crowns
> [her/him] with victory.

> The Lord set his affection on _____ and loved
> [her/him].

Does taking these truths of God and applying them directly to yourself seem like sacrilege? Dear friend, if you struggle to put your name into these promises, then you need this rewrite. Think about inserting your name and then posting these verses on your bathroom mirror or your car dashboard. Consider reading them—personalized—out loud every single day for a month. Let God rewrite your story and experience the incredible peace and joy that comes from knowing your security in Jesus Christ.

When you live from your new story, you can be both rigorously honest and gentle with yourself. It's possible because of who God is and how He defines us. Thomas Merton once wrote that "the man who is not afraid to admit everything that he sees to be wrong with himself, and yet recognizes that he may be the object of God's love precisely because of his shortcomings, can begin to be sincere. His sincerity is based on confidence, not in his illusions about himself, but in the endless, unfailing mercy of God."[5]

It's possible to see the wrong in ourselves and be sincere and confident in Christ. We can be honest *and* loving with ourselves. Our inner voices soften and shift as we begin to see ourselves as loved by God rather than as people who must meet certain standards to be worthy of love. And when that shift happens, everything around us begins to change.

Rewriting Our Relationships with Others

The default setting of our hearts is self-centered. In some ways, dealing with people from our own self-centered perspective is natural. Child development psychologist Jean Piaget referred to this stage of development as "egocentrism." It is natural for young children to be able to see the world only from their point of view, and to assume that everyone around them perceives the world exactly as they do. By age eight, children who are developing in healthy ways begin to develop empathy, but unfortunately, I've known many adults decades older who have never grasped the concept of others-centered perspectives. I know I'm still learning how to develop such a perspective! Perhaps we are all seven-year-olds on the inside, still surprised that our point of view is not *the* point of view.

Once we allow God to begin rewriting our stories with the language of love, however, we can begin to use words to build others up as well. In a call to others-centered living, Hebrews 6:1 admonishes us to "move beyond the elementary teachings about Christ and be taken forward to maturity." Learning to develop a new foundation for how we communicate with others is a sign of maturity. The book of Proverbs characterizes the difference between wise and foolish people—and it's most obvious in their speech. The way we use words *for* or *against* one another will reveal our inner strength of character. As God is at work rewriting our stories, the foundational way we engage with the people we are closest to changes. The way we use words with others should shift in three key ways: humility, sincerity, and grace.

Humility

When approaching a conversation or conflict with humility, our attitude should reflect the following motivations:

- *I desire to know the whole story from the other person's perspective before I make any assumptions about what's happened.*
- *There's a good chance I am wrong about some part of this story.*
- *I am open to receiving this person's perspective on how I contributed to this conflict/issue.*
- *I am willing to grow through this interaction.*

There's no greater training ground for humility than the emotionally laden text message. Recently I texted my friend about an event she had committed to. Almost immediately, she responded with, "I can't do it."

My natural response was, *What the heck? You just committed two days ago!*

I picked up my phone and typed in a snappy reply, only to take a deep breath before hitting send. Then I deleted it.

Humility stops us from sending such texts. When we

desire to grow in our wholehearted loving, we will need self-control and a teachable spirit. Repeatedly, Proverbs warns us to not become fools by acting out of pride (*How dare you change your plans!*) or speaking impulsively (*I'll send that hasty retort!*).

A fool's mouth lashes out with pride.
PROVERBS 14:3

Every fool is quick to quarrel.
PROVERBS 20:3

Do you see a person wise in their own eyes? There is more hope for a fool than for them.
PROVERBS 26:12

Generally, if we struggle with humility, we struggle with self-awareness because if we knew who we really are, we wouldn't be so high on ourselves! When we actually do a rigorous self-inventory of our own shortcomings, when we allow the truth of who we are to drive us toward Christ's forgiveness and mercy, we grow in humility. It often takes a painful understanding of our own sin—not just one time, but time and time again—to break us of our pride. It's painful, but it's a good pain. The point of that pain is not to move us toward condemnation or shame but toward growth and freedom.

Only those who have been broken can treat others' brokenness with gentleness. Perhaps you don't struggle with fear, so your first response is to get annoyed with people who do. But when you tell yourself, *I might not struggle with anxiety like Suzy does, but I do struggle with pride [or anger or lust], so I will be gentle with Suzy in her struggle.* You may need to intentionally speak to yourself like this when you find yourself becoming annoyed with someone as a means of coaching yourself into sincerity and grace.

Sincerity

"Love must be sincere. Hate what is evil; cling to what is good" (Romans 12:9). In Scripture, the Greek word used for *sincere* actually means "inexperienced in the art of acting."[6] To be sincere with our words means to avoid massaging, editing, and working words in our favor. To be sincere is to relentlessly refuse to say one thing and mean another. To be sincere is to take our loved ones at their word, to seek to make sure we fully understand what they mean, and then to move confidently forward *believing they mean what they say.* To be sincere is to make sure *we also say what we believe and stick to it—with an emphasis on humility and grace.*

If you struggle to speak honestly and plainly about your failings, needs, or hurts, it will take practice to be sincere when communicating with others. It will also take self-control and discipline to stick with what you've said, and it will take courage to revisit a conversation if you know you weren't sincere.

Sincerity means that when you apologize, you do not resurrect your hurt the next time you argue with your loved one. To be sincere means that you seek to find the words to communicate your own feelings and do not try to resolve arguments so quickly that you don't even know what's behind the argument in the first place. To be sincere requires much practice in the discipline of listening and asking honest and vulnerable questions.

In my previous example with the text interchange, to be sincere would mean picking up the phone (crazy, I know!) and asking my friend, "Hey, it seems like you might have been overwhelmed when you sent that text. I'm calling to see if everything's okay."

To be sincere always takes more tact, more work, more care. Maybe that's why Romans 12:9 says, "Love must be sincere." Love always chooses to move toward people with genuine concern, rather than away from them with sarcastic, manipulative, or hypocritical words.

Grace

Finally, as we seek to redeem our relationships with others, we will speak from a heart of grace, which is the culmination of humility and sincerity. Grace enables us to incline our hearts toward reconciliation and forgiveness. Gracious words are proactive and specific, and they are often used when we encourage or apologize to others. Encouraging words build confidence; words of apology repair damage. Both are mandatory and necessary nearly every day of our lives.

Encouraging words build confidence; words of apology repair damage.

Encouraging words of grace come when we speak words of healing and love. What if you invited God to be with you as you gave specific encouragement and feedback every day? Words change lives. We are often unaware of how our specific words of encouragement are doing a healing work in someone's soul. We are not privy to their whole past or the stories they are tempted to believe, but we can be part of God's healing and redeeming work through the words we share.

If you want to feel God in your life, make an intentional effort to have eyes to see specific ways you can encourage someone. Encouragement is best when it highlights an immediate action that speaks to a deeper virtue. If you catch your children being gentle with one another, you can encourage them about the men or women of patience you see them becoming. If you notice an employee taking an extra step in her work, you can encourage her about the qualities of leadership that you've noticed in her actions. You will be in the middle of God's work if you are in the middle of healing words.

On the repair side, as a person of grace, you seek forgiveness when you've made a mistake or hurt someone. Such words of grace should also be proactively specific. No one should be better at giving apologies than the Christian. Because you've been loved, saved, and healed by grace, you can fully accept your failings and apologize. True words of apology have several characteristics: They are specific about how one has wronged the other; the words don't include language that expects an apology in return (public service announcement: if you are apologizing only to draw an apology from the other, *you aren't actually apologizing*), and true apologies seek to reconcile hearts as the main goal. I've written at length about the process and power of forgiveness in both *She's Got Issues* and *Brave Enough*, and I refer you to those chapters for a deeper discussion of growth in forgiveness.[7]

Finally, you will find your relationships with others being rewritten into a new and redeemed story as you grow in these five foundational ways:

1. *Cultivate curiosity.* Make your conversations about the other people. Ask questions to understand them. If this is new for a relationship you've been in for a long time (like family and marriage), be patient with the process. Sometimes sincerity is seen as suspect until it's proven genuine over time. For some people in your life, such conversations will be so different from those in their other relationships that it might take them a while to warm up to your real interest in them. And if you aren't sincerely interested in them, ask God to give you the love you are lacking. It is in line with God's nature to answer that prayer.

2. *Avoid sarcasm.* At its core, sarcasm is veiled contempt. Sarcasm stands opposite of sincerity because it uses words to convey underlying meaning. Sarcasm is "made to criticize someone . . . in a way that is amusing to others but annoying to the person criticized."[8] If you find yourself resorting to sarcasm, pause to internally check yourself: What are you really feeling? What are you struggling to convey? Are you using someone

to make yourself look or feel better? If necessary, take a break from the conversation and seek to understand what's really going on with you.

3. *Be a generous listener.* Author and broadcaster Krista Tippett defines this ability as "a kind of vulner-ability—a willingness to be surprised, to let go of assumptions and take in ambiguity. The listener wants to understand the humanity behind the words of the other, and patiently summons one's own best self and one's own best words and questions."[9] A generous listener uses a fond regard for the other person and genuine questions to make discoveries—to help both people discover new things about themselves and the world. A generous listener seeks to fully understand the other before expressing his or her own view.

4. *Develop compassion and capacity for brokenness.* There are a few evil people in the world. There are some fools who will never learn. But every single person— good or evil, foolish or wise—every single one has been wounded by the four-way brokenness in this world. The better we understand this, the more likely we are to see the similarities between ourselves and others, regardless of how different our way of life or beliefs might be. It is always the enemy's work to divide, so he will always seek to highlight "dividing" issues. We know he has succeeded when we believe

that a difficult person in our lives is against us and that the divide between us is a chasm too deep and too wide to cross. This is the rallying cry of darkness that Christ proved a lie on the cross.

Christ Himself is our peace, and that peace was achieved when "in his own body on the cross, he broke down the wall of hostility that separated us" (Ephesians 2:14, NLT). Our knowledge about Jesus becomes action in Jesus when we recognize the divisive words in our marriages, families, and workplaces as direct attacks from an enemy who desires to divide us. One of the most powerful ways victory in Christ is lived out is in our willingness to resolve conflict with our loved ones with humility and compassion. Incredible, but true. Christ is most magnified in the small, selfless choices of men and women who choose to believe in the unifying love of Christ over the dividing power of the flesh.

Christ is most magnified in the small, selfless choices of men and women who choose to believe in the unifying love of Christ over the dividing power of the flesh.

5. *Learn the stories you are tempted to believe.* Human beings are quick learners. We instinctively learn from experience and rely on those lessons to make conclusions in future situations. Author and psychologist Brené Brown points out that our brains are hardwired

for stories. Recognizing the power of narratives, our brains reward us for providing explanations for what has happened to us, whether those stories are accurate or not.[10]

The reason we need to retrace our old stories before we can live in the new one is that our brains will hijack our desire to live differently by returning us to those old conclusions, again and again. Each of us has certain story lines we are tempted to believe. Whenever you enter into a conversation or conflict and notice that you are responding with more intensity than the situation itself requires, you have likely fallen into an old story line. *Listen to the story.* The more familiar you are with your old stories, the more equipped you will be to avoid typecasting new situations and new people into old, painful stories.

Recently, I needed to call someone I work with and explain that the project I was completing was going to be turned in with some major changes. I found myself hesitant to make the call. I waited two days, telling myself, *I need to pray about this first.* I did pray about it, but mostly I just talked to myself about it for a while—and then realized I was following the script from my old story. Here's how it sounded:

> *When I call her, I don't know what's going to happen next. What if she doesn't like my idea? What if she tells me that I need to go back and*

revisit all those changes? I don't have the strength to do that, and I think I'm right. I didn't do what I said I was going to do so she's going to think that I'm high maintenance. I'm going to make her work harder. She's going to be mad at me.

Once I paid attention to my self-talk, I was able to read the story line somewhat objectively and ask myself, *Is this true?* When I did, I remembered the conversations I've had with this person when she's told me she loves my work. I remembered how hard we've worked together in the past. Asking myself, *Is my expectation the rule or the exception?* helped move me away from the temptation to believe the old story line. When I looked for the truth outside this one moment, God reminded me that I don't have to live from the fake story that *everyone is against me.*

I called my coworker. I told her I was worried about her response because her opinion is important to me. She responded to my honesty with her own sincerity. She was open and generous with the new idea. She was compassionate about the work. I had almost believed a fake story, and in doing so, I would have missed out on the chance to grow into a deeper, more trusting relationship with my coworker. The old story lines die hard. Yes, rewriting the script of our hearts is hard work, but it's the best kind of work we can ever do.

Rewriting Our Relationship with the World

During creation, God established rhythms of worship and celebration for people within the land and the work they were given. Yet our society has rapidly shifted to a disconnected stance from our place in the earth. We have lost our "earthiness."

The role of technology in our disconnection is fascinating and disturbing. We all know that our electronic devices are potent tools that are not evil in themselves—they're just powerful. Power can always be used for both good and evil. However, one of the most devious parts of technology is its ability to lure us into thinking we are more connected to others, even as we detach more and more from the specific place (physically and relationally) where God has placed us. Technology can isolate us into a self-created world where we have complete control over the words—the words about the relationships we pursue, the news we read, and the "truth" we experience. If that becomes our primary source of reality, we will lose our grounding in our relationship with the greater world.

My whole family recently took a trip to South Africa to visit some friends who'd moved there. This was the trip of a lifetime—a huge experience for our kids, Dave, and me as we navigated a multicontinent flight and our children's first trip outside of the United States. One of our greatest takeaways from those ten days was how *grounded* our South African friends were within their community. Meals were not transactional experiences but the unhurried setting for pursuing meaningful conversation. We noticed that people in lines at the grocery store, at bus stops, and in their cars were not on their devices, but were just "being." When we returned from that trip, I was stunned at the number of people I observed looking at their phones in every facet of daily life—in grocery lines, waiting rooms, the workplace, restaurants, cars, sports practices, the gym, even the restroom! It may seem like a simple truth, but we need to remember that when we jump into our own technology portals, we leave the reality we've been grounded within. Our awareness shifts from the world around us to the world we've created. Over time, it becomes dangerous to live only within the world we've created on a personal-sized screen.

To rewrite our stories, we must pay particular attention to the world right in front of us, as well as to the larger world. Theologian Karl Barth said, "Take your Bible and take your newspaper, and read both. But interpret newspapers from your Bible."[11] To deal with our world with a sense of settled activism—neither dissolving into fearful hysterics nor hardening our hearts behind walls of comfort and privilege—we will need to intentionally manage the way we engage. We will need to become students of both worlds, seeking God's direction for our role when we pray "your kingdom come."

Our willingness to submit to our place within creation leads to a fruitful and abundant life. As the prophet Isaiah said, God promises that "if you are willing and obedient, you will eat the good things of the land" (Isaiah 1:19). Our attentiveness to our place in the created world will slowly bring about a shift in our perspective from cynicism to wonder, from anxiousness to peace. The simple act of taking notice of everything bigger than you—the trees, the sun and moon, the rolling hills, the wide rivers—can shift your perspective off yourself and back onto the Creator.

Through the prophet Isaiah, God also speaks of our role in bringing restoration to the earth as we pursue the things He cares deeply about: "Stop doing wrong. Learn to do right; seek justice. Defend the oppressed. Take up the cause of the fatherless; plead the case of the widow" (Isaiah 1:16-17). Of course, sometimes it's easier to profess our love and passion for those far away than it is to actually act in love and passion for those close by. Yet we cannot care for one and not the other.

It is only when we understand our "earthiness" that we can understand our call to activism. In her book on wisdom, Krista Tippett quotes "wise woman and physician"[12] Rachel Naomi Remen, who shared a story her grandfather had told her as a child, profoundly shaping her experience with the world. In the story, the whole world was created in light but was shattered into fragments that are now hidden everywhere. Her grandfather explained the role of humanity through the story:

> We are here because we are born with the capacity to find the hidden light in all events and all people, to lift it up and make it visible once again and thereby to restore the innate wholeness of the world. It's a very important story for our times.

This task is called *tikkun olam* in Hebrew. It's the restoration of the world.

And this is, of course, a collective task. It involves all people who have ever been born. . . . We are all healers of the world. . . . It's not about healing the world by making a huge difference. It's about healing the world that touches you, that's around you.

The world to which you have proximity.[13]

Jesus, through whom all things were created, is the restoring Light of the World.[14] We illuminate Him in every act of cultivation and moment of wonder in the world around us, every act of justice and encouragement done through us, every act that redeems something broken or reconciles disconnected people. The way we move through the world is the culmination of God's redeeming story in our hearts. As we discover new words and new story lines, we live with a deep settledness and hope. We live with wonder and with an expectant heart toward God's direction in us and to us. It is only within this story that we can live into Jesus' words to us: "You are the light of the world" (Matthew 5:14).

Our four-way brokenness becomes four-way redemption, one word at a time.

Keeping It Real

1. Most of us have been impacted by both good and bad words in our old stories. What are some of the words, beliefs, or images that still affect you today?

2. When it comes to your internal language about God and yourself, where do you need a rewrite?

3. In what areas of your life have you grown in your relationship with others? Where do you still need to grow?

4. How do you understand God's work in the world? How do you understand your role in God's work?

10

The Chapters
Ending Well

The unexamined life is not worth living.

SOCRATES

The inspiration for this final chapter—of both this book and of the foundations for our new stories—comes from a source I didn't expect.

As I finish writing this book, it is my last summer in my thirties. I've been surprised by the level of reflection and intensity that accompanied this benchmark birthday. I've always been the young one—in my parenting, in my group of friends, in my work. I hurried through college and gradu-ate school, marriage, and children, always rushing to the next stage. Now I find myself digging in my heels, wishing time would slow down a bit so I could sit down and think.

With this summer of reflection, I've renewed my

commitment to working out, partially motivated by a desire to be whole and healthy and partially motivated by my longing to push off the inevitable creep of middle age and pretend I'm still twenty-five. Somehow, being thirty-nine makes me imagine being seventy-nine, in a wheelchair complaining about the rubbery eggs for breakfast and bemoaning how tired I am. So while working on this book, I've been spending more time in the gym, a place I like to go to about as much as I like going to the dentist to get a cavity filled.

My survival mechanism at the gym is to read magazines featuring mind-numbing stories like "Sexy New Purse Styles That Will Change Your Life" or "Three Ways to Update Your Summer Hair." One day, though, while scanning the rack, a cover story on "rewriting your love story" caught my eye. I began my trek on the elliptical while flipping through the magazine, dropping inserts and making the area reek of perfume samples. When I turned to the page promising a love rewrite, I was surprised by what I found. The article was about the true story that inspired the movie *The Big Sick*—an American woman (Emily) and a Pakistani man (Kumail) fall in love despite cultural differences. But the story wasn't really about those differences; it was a story of how their love for each other solidified when Emily developed a rare illness and was put into a medically induced coma.[1]

This was a story about life and death, about love and commitment, about what really matters. In the middle of reading a pop-culture magazine in a smelly gym where I was trying to flee my inevitable aging, I was reminded that our world is shaped with meaning by the surprising and unwelcome circumstances of transitions, suffering, and even death.

In his book *Walking with God through Pain and Suffering*, author and pastor Tim Keller reminds his readers about the truth of the human condition:

> Tens of thousands of people die every day in unexpected tragedies, and hundreds of thousands around them are crushed by grief and shock. The majority of them trigger no headlines because pain and misery is the norm in this world. . . . *Nothing is more important than to learn how to maintain a life of purpose in the midst of painful adversity.*[2]

Or, as my friend Pete said when beginning a sermon: "In other words, nothing is more important than to make sense of suffering."

I think the vitality of our souls is at risk when we give in to the temptation to live a superficial existence, to flee from the painful moments and difficult questions that often create meaning. Living day to day in the topsoil of our souls will create shallow roots that cannot sustain us when the inevitable seasons of transition and grief plow into our lives. When our lives demand depth—when we move from struggle into suffering, when we enter into places of confusion and doubt, when sorrow and pain come to us in the form of death and grief—will our roots be strong enough so that we can stand firm? Will we be a "planting of the LORD for the display of his splendor" (Isaiah 61:3), or will we be like the shoots in

Jesus' parable that were choked out, unfruitful because of the worries of this world (Mark 4:19)?

The painful confusion that transitions and endings bring will always challenge our ability to live into our new stories. Transitions shake our foundation, testing its integrity. When our footing becomes unstable, we are more likely to derail out of the freedom cycle, turning back to old ways of living rather than digging deeper into the new story. At the core, transitions are times when decisions are required. *Is it time to quit this job? Is this the end of the relationship? Should I take my child to see that counselor? How will our marriage make it?* Transitions often bring new beginnings, but also inevitably force endings, which bring their own kind of surprising grief as we lose what's familiar and have to reckon with our own emotions of uncertainty.

Endings come in many forms. Some endings are the result of our own decisions. *It's a new opportunity. I'm going back to school. I'm moving out.* Harder endings come to us unbidden. *My best friend moved. My job is being eliminated. Dad is getting remarried. The doctor called with the test results.* Endings bring life as we know it to a jarring halt. Suddenly our new stories are challenged. We wonder if we are enough. We wonder if God is really present. And even more—we wonder how God could allow such deep pain if He cares for us.

Transitions and endings don't include only the obvious life changes like divorce (which we assume we won't need to think about) or death (which we act like won't come to us). But how we interpret the meaning of the big changes will impact the meaning we assign to little changes.

Moses, no stranger to hardship, prayed that God would "teach us to number our days aright, that we may gain a heart of wisdom" (Psalm 90:12). In other words, he asked for God's help to face pain head-on. Today we live in a world filled with powerful distractions designed to help us numb, escape from, or buy our way out of harsh reality. Facing loss in our lives squarely and honestly—refusing the anesthesia of superficial living and choosing to know life fully—has surprising benefits to the way we experience our ordinary days. To number our days aright changes the story we tell ourselves when the road gets dark and we can't see the next turn. Instead of veering off the freedom cycle and away from truth, love, and forgiveness, "numbering our days aright" teaches us to lean into God's love and our identity as His beloved children.

I learned how much transitions impact us through a recent experience with my friend Megan. Megan and her husband were entering a new season. She would say that they chose this transition, but it also somehow chose them. After months of discernment and prayer, our friends were becoming missionaries, leaving the community of their childhood and embarking on an adventure nine thousand miles away. Although they planned on this being a temporary move—maybe two years—it still required a complete overhaul. They sold everything they had and raised their own salaries, and after a few months of that weird transition when one wonders if the next chapter is really coming, they had their plane tickets and their friends had planned the good-bye party. The ending was becoming real.

During this "waiting around to leave" period, Megan and I went for a run through the rolling hills of the one community she's known her whole life. We chatted about the usual topics—family, friends, and the last-minute logistics of the trip. Then Megan got quiet. I took a sidelong glance at her and realized she was crying. I reached for her arm, and we both stopped. This quiet, confident, and faithful young woman began to cry harder—deep, full sobs—leaning over and letting the tears come in wave after wave. And in the middle of the neighborhood on a beautiful autumn morning, surrounded by creation singing of change in colors of deep green, blazing red, and warm orange, I think Megan let herself feel the end.

She confessed her own ambivalence. She wanted to trust God with this next step but felt confused and distressed by all the unfinished business around her. She was leaving behind a number of stories that hadn't been resolved—strained relationships, toxic family patterns, and the confusion and doubt that had crept into her own story. An ending to a chapter in her life dredged up all the other endings—the ones Megan sensed were coming in difficult struggles that she wasn't quite sure how to interpret. Megan was stuck between her stories—the old story screaming loudly from her past, bringing up all the ways she wasn't going to be safe, secure, or loved in this new chapter.

What do we do when we face transitions—the ones we choose and the ones we don't? How do we navigate pain when we enter unfamiliar territory? How do we stay true to our new stories when it would be easier to fall back into old patterns? How do we rewrite our lives when the plot takes an unexpected turn?

Unfinished Business

There's a story in the Bible that speaks of this kind of unfinished business. The passage centers on a woman who comes alone at midday to draw water at a well. No doubt she is surprised to find Jesus sitting there when she arrives. She is even more shocked when He, a Jewish rabbi, engages her, a Samaritan woman, in conversation. (Jews and Samaritans did not get along and certainly did not engage in meaningful conversations.) Jesus begins to talk with her about living water—water that can quench her soul thirst, the deep places in her that are parched and arid and dry. She's guarded—but intrigued. So Jesus makes their abstract conversation really personal by asking her to get her husband to join them. She deflects His question by answering with a true (kind of) answer: "I have no husband" (John 4:17).

Jesus then shows just a peek of His own divine cards by answering, "The fact is, you have had five husbands, and the man you now have is not your husband. What you have just said is quite true" (John 4:18). Still not knowing to whom she's speaking, the Samaritan woman sidelines the truth by arguing about the legalities of where she's allowed to worship as a "less than" Samaritan.

This is a woman of unfinished business, one whose story feels broken on so many levels.

Most Bible commentators categorize her as a bad woman.

She's failed at five marriages and presumably been divorced that many times. She's now living with a man—and if that would be unseemly in your church today, imagine how scandalous it would have been in ancient Samaria! Some Bible commentators describe her life as "exceedingly immoral."[3] The rest of the story's details are interpreted through this bad-woman lens. Her sinful life becomes the reason she travels so far to the well, the reason she's alone, the reason she draws water at noon. The bad-woman story makes her life her own fault. The bad-woman story is the reason she needs Jesus to serve up some truth alongside her living water.

There's another camp of interpreters who look at this story a bit differently. In this camp, the Samaritan woman is a tragic figure in a sad story. These commentators point out that a first-century woman had virtually no marital rights (although a Jewish man could divorce his wife even over a poorly cooked meal), so the idea that *she* is the one who left her husbands is preposterous. Moreover, a woman who has been married five times is more likely to be widowed than to be an adulteress. Because men represented provision and protection, a woman whose husband died would have an immediate, pressing need to find another man who would offer her that same security—hence the serial marriages.

To add one more twist to the tragic plot, if the woman is now living with a man who's not her husband, perhaps she's been forced to serve as a second or third woman in a household, to accept the role of concubine because no one else would take her in. In this version of the story, the woman is a living tragedy. Her life is a series of unfortunate events because she is the victim of circumstance—unable to control her story in any way. In this story line, we have pity on her and see Jesus as compassionate because of her circumstances. But even that doesn't fully capture the extent of God's love through Jesus. We want to explain why Jesus reacts—with truth if she's "bad"; with grace if she's "sad."

But the reality is that Jesus is the perfect picture of *both* grace and truth. Although our human tendency is to want to place this woman—and ourselves—in a bad/sad category when it comes to unfinished and painful business, the reality is that most of our lives are colored in gray scale. Some parts are bad, some are sad, and we all need the loving grace and truth that Jesus brings.

Because of our desire to make sense of the pain and suffering in our world, we look for the right chapters to place these stories in. When we enter into our own unfinished business, we try out the guilt story: *Was this my fault? Why is this happening? What have I done to bring this on? Am I bad?* If guilt doesn't fit, we might move into a chapter of victimization and anger: *Is God in this? Why would a good God allow me to feel this much pain? Am I a tragedy that God has forgotten? Why isn't this resolved? Where is my happy ending?*

When the chapters don't go as we planned, we often become unmoored by what we can't control. We are tempted to wallow in self-pity and to turn back to the temporary comforts we used in our old stories to control the painful emotions of grief that we didn't see coming.

The Samaritan woman tried to deflect Jesus' probing questions, but He didn't want to talk about superficialities. He went right to the truth of her unfinished business so He could lead her into deeper places—into places of greater meaning.

When Megan started crying on our run, it wasn't because she was overwhelmed by her packing list. She was overwhelmed by the deeper places where life didn't make sense and she didn't know how to end one chapter and move on to the next.

Unfinished business is like this. It defies categories. Endings in our stories are never all bad or all sad. Threads of sadness, anger, disappointment, loneliness, and fear become a tightly wound ball of loss sitting in the middle of our chest, bulky and burdensome. As a result, we feel like we can't take a deep breath or see beyond this massive tangle of negative emotion.

Healthy guilt is a sign of a wrong we've committed that needs to be made right. Healthy grief is the response to unfinished business that we can't control.

Our world doesn't make much room for complexity like this. We don't make much space for grief, so we tend to mistake grief for guilt. We believe the lie that there is more we could have done, more we should be. We believe that our perfection would make the world perfect. But there's a difference between guilt and grief. Healthy guilt is a sign of a wrong we've committed that needs to be made right. Healthy grief is the response to unfinished business that we can't control. Grief is the natural response to losses of all kinds—a loss of the relationships we thought we could reconcile; the loss of a life that we expected we would have; the loss of security, comfort, or control when we step out in faith.

As much as we might dislike it, there is a time for the grief that comes during transitions. "For everything there is a season, a time for every activity under heaven" (Ecclesiastes 3:1, NLT). There is a time for seasons to change. There is a time for the conflicting feelings and the dizzying circles of loss that come with the end of something—the loss of a loved one; the loss of a familiar home, job, or season of life. Endings even bring with them a sense of a loss of a piece of ourselves—something in us that had attached to another thing or person. So to describe grief as a "sharp sorrow" is accurate, as a piece of us is cut away. In my conflicted feelings last summer, grief felt like losing the piece of myself that had identified as young and "on the fast track." Grief looked like letting those feelings come, giving space in my soul to allow those feelings to live and be named, and then gently letting them go. For some seasons, this takes just a moment or a day. For others, the process is much longer.

Perhaps you can immediately think of a clear chapter of sorrow in your own life—perhaps the death of your innocence or the untimely death of a loved one. When people describe losing their father to suicide or losing their innocence to abuse, we try to cut a wide swath of space for that sadness, to give room for that conflicting ball of emotion. But even those of us who haven't suffered such enormous tragedy have lives punctuated by other kinds of loss, endings that don't fit as well into one clear story line. We often don't fully acknowledge the suffering those losses cause. We categorize them as not serious enough for grief and deny our souls the space they need to express the nuances of sorrow and to bring meaning to the suffering.

To live wholeheartedly, however, is impossible without a brave face-to-face relationship with loss. To gain a heart of wisdom requires us to number our days aright—to take the good and the bad, the beginnings and the endings, the births and the deaths—and allow space for God to write His story within it all. Letting go of my youthfulness last summer was a prerequisite to the birth of a new season—a time I'm just beginning to enjoy, in which I feel a new sense of responsibility to steward my influence for the good of my family, my church, and my community. If I clung tightly to the old, there wouldn't be room in my heart for this new chapter. It's a different chapter—but it's *good*.

So we end our journey together with some stories— stories of transition, stories of growth, stories of grief. Each of these stories was written by a friend of mine—someone who has taught me incredible things because he or she has lived through painful—even excruciating—circumstances and is now living in a redeemed story. Not a happy story, necessarily. Not a perfect story. But a story of depth, meaning, and purpose.

The Bible speaks to us about Jesus as our Living Word. We find Him in the pages of Scripture, and we find Him in the pages of our new stories—in Brianna's, in Lisa's, in Tommy's, in yours, and in mine.

* * *

There's something special about being a part of someone's life in their twenties. This decade is full of potential and possibility. Young adulthood is often the first time that we truly must reckon with our stories and make the intentional choice to move toward God and His way. Brianna has taught me so much about the power of honesty and vulnerability, even in really difficult times. Watching her be transformed by something that the world would call irredeemable was nothing short of a miracle. But I'll let her tell you the rest . . .

Brianna's Story

My story begins on the day that I could no longer put on a happy face. It had been nine months since my husband had made a devastating confession to me that impacted our marriage, and I was still hurting. I had run out of good vibes, out of positive thinking, and to be frank, out of hope. In fact, I felt worse nine months later than I had right after getting the news. I found myself face-to-face with questions I never imagined having to ask myself: Should I leave my husband? Is this even worth it?

When my friend asked how I was doing, I admitted I wasn't happy. I didn't want to be with my husband after what had happened. I told her that if I was going to leave, I'd better leave then, before it was too late. As a Christian, I thought I only had a certain window of time post-trauma for divorce to be justifiable. I was absolutely in the pit. I'd spent those first nine months surviving and coming to terms with a situation I never wanted. Now I realized it was time to live, and to do so I needed to reconcile the strain I was living under. God prompted me to pursue counseling—if there was any shot of rebuilding my marriage, I would need some professional support.

What I learned about God during that time is that He is absolutely with us in the pain. I can look back and see how the circumstances that made me feel so trapped were actually keeping me still, keeping me on the right path. I'm a runner (not literally, of course—as they say, if you see me actually running, call the police). I run from pain and boredom. But those initial circumstances trapped me, and I couldn't run. I thought that meant God was far from me, but in fact, He was so close. Of course, betrayal isn't His intent for marriage; however, in the midst of my pain, He wept with me. Through relationships and circumstances, He provided empathy, support, and the strength I needed to get from one day to the next.

For the first time, I also understood grace. Holy cow. Grace given and grace received. My people didn't flinch in our shame and our strife. They loved, cared, and provided for our needs. So it is with God.

As for me, I learned I could stay in this—with the help of Jesus and Jesus-loving friends. Alone, no way. In community, absolutely. There's no formula for conquering hard things in life. Some of life's most insurmountable events come unplanned, and I learned that I could do it without a plan. One single day at a time. I learned so much perspective. Suddenly, life's trivial obsessions disappeared. I also learned my painful circumstances aren't my identity. I did not need to wear the shame and abandonment I felt through this marriage crisis on my chest like a scarlet letter. I learned this is not who I am. In Christ, I am not forsaken. In Christ, I am free from the guilt and the shame. I look to Him and I am radiant.

Looking back, I'm not sure I would do a lot differently. When first thinking about this, I thought, well maybe I would have gotten individual counseling sooner or would have done something else sooner or better. We always feel like we should've done better, right?

But actually looking back I think, nope, I did what I knew to do. I took things one day at a time. I set the bar lower—not because my life wasn't worth it, but because when all else faded and I was just with Jesus in my circumstances, the societal pressures were meaningless. Not much else mattered but walking in grace and truth day in and day out. As someone who was already following Jesus (which is why our marital problems seemed so out of left field for us), I could be confident that I was not alone. I could take care of my daughter, myself, and life's responsibilities as I relied on the Lord. I already had enough pain to concern myself with without thinking I "should've" done this or "could've" done that. As my counselor said in our initial marriage intensive, stop "should-ing" on yourself.

Almost instantly people told us our marriage would be better than it started, and let me tell you, I didn't believe them for a second. I'd kindly smile and nod, but I couldn't fathom it. Fortunately, turns out they were right. After putting in work together and individually, my husband and I began a rhythm of vulnerability and honesty in our marriage instead of our old way of communicating with walls up. We're jiving and connecting better than we ever have now that we've trudged through really hard, exposing things together. I'm now able to trust a man who leads well and with integrity. I'm proud of him. I'm not ashamed of where we've been because I'm thankful to share how God's actual grace and love continue to lead us into healing. And here's the thing: Our lives haven't gotten a lot easier in terms of our circumstances. We're wrestling with our calling and purpose while trying to pay off big debts and raising three little kids. My husband is busy with full-time work and full-time seminary courses. The difference now is that we're letting these things bring us toward each other rather than pull us apart.

To someone facing transition, I would say: Call on Jesus. Just choose to know Him. Literally just say His name each day, each moment. That continual acknowledgment will move you toward relying on Him and seeking Him—living above crisis mode. I'd also say be vulnerable. Rely on godly women to support you. They will. Don't isolate yourself in pain. Speak out your pain—your hurt and your fear. We cannot walk through this alone; we weren't meant to. We can never experience grace if we never allow our true selves to be known. It's scary, but it's the best thing ever. And man, oh man, will your life, your story, and your healing be a light and a comfort to those experiencing hardship in life.

* * *

Brianna's story is an example of someone allowing a deeply painful struggle in her marriage to become the first chapter in an entirely new beginning for both her and her husband. Hers is a story of hope and redemption—but hope and redemption don't always look the same.

That's why it was important to me to include not just Brianna's story here, but Lisa's as well. I first met Lisa at a leadership retreat a couple of summers ago. I admired her quick wit, her strategic thinking, and her depth of wisdom. (The fact that she also has amazing style didn't hurt either!) As we began to unpack our stories, it was clear that Lisa had found herself in an unexpected chapter. Over the course of the next two years, our friendship grew even as Lisa experienced several challenging endings—and she began to live into her new season.

Lisa's Story

At age twenty-nine, I walked down the aisle to the song "Beautiful Things": "You make beautiful things out of the dust, out of us." On my wedding day, I believed that marriage would be hard but that if I trusted in the Lord enough and was really committed, then I'd be married "'til death do us part." That's what people do. At least that's what good Christians do. I'd grown up in church, and my parents are still married after thirty-five years.

It took only six months for me to realize that marriage was going to be much harder than I'd ever imagined. I was on staff at a large church, serving in a very visible role. I was terrified to tell anyone about my marital problems. I spent years smiling and telling people I was okay, my marriage was great, and everything was okay! But I was definitely not okay, my marriage was not great, and things were not okay.

My husband and I went to counseling off and on for years, seeing multiple therapists, hoping someone would help us fix the problems in our marriage. I read all the marriage books; I tried everything I could think of. And I spent years begging God for a miracle, praying, hoping something would change. I'd lie in bed at night, feeling like the walls were closing in on me, sometimes feeling physically unable to breathe. I could not see a way out. My marriage was definitely not honoring to God, but I didn't believe a divorce would be honoring to Him either. I was afraid of losing my career in ministry. I felt very trapped. Verse 4 of Psalm 18 states that "the cords of death entangled me." That might seem a bit dramatic, but there were dark moments when I felt that death would have been a better option than my life.

I remember very vividly God bringing another verse from Psalm 18 to mind late one night: "He brought me out into a spacious place; he rescued me because he delighted in me" (verse 19). I clung to the image of a spacious place. It was at times quite literally a lifeline.

And then, after days and months and years—four years to be exact—I came to the sad realization that I just couldn't do it anymore. Our marriage had a level of unhealthiness and toxicity that I could not overcome on my own. My issues with my husband were not "I hate that he squeezes the toothpaste tube in the middle" or "he watches too much football on Sundays" or even "I'm just not happy." There were ongoing, unrepentant patterns of behavior taking place, and I knew I had to leave.

Since I was serving on a church staff, I had to walk through a process with church leaders, elders, and my faith community. While they affirmed that I should remain in ministry, I wrestled with a lot of guilt and self-blame. I still do today.

Now living on the other side of this, I'd encourage someone in a similar situation to invite safe people to be a witness to your marriage, even if it's painful and terrifying. They'll pray with and for you. At the right times, they'll be the ones to encourage you to keep going, try something else, or find another counselor. Or in the end they will say, "There really is nothing else you can do." When I'm filled with doubt and think, Was it really that bad? *I call them. They tell me, "We were there. We prayed with you; we cried with you, grieved with you. You did everything you could." I'm incredibly grateful for those people today.*

One of my biggest fears walking through a divorce was that God would be done with me. That somehow I'd made such a mess of things that He wouldn't be able to use me in ministry anymore. Perhaps you find yourself feeling stuck, like the walls are closing in. You're not feeling okay. And that's okay.

Going through a divorce revealed a lot of doubt and false beliefs that were baked into the foundation of my faith. I believed that if I did all the right things, then life would work out great for me. I'd have a happy marriage and raise a family, take the kids to Disneyland, get a dog. Right now, all I have to show for it is the dog.

I still believe in the sacredness of the covenant of marriage and believe God intends it to last a lifetime. And I still believe God has the power to heal any marriage or broken relationship. I've seen Him do that in big, miraculous ways for other people throughout my life. And I so desperately wanted that to be my story as well. But for whatever reason, it wasn't. And that's part of the "not okayness" of all this. I live with the reality that "God can, but He didn't."

As I was coming to terms with the end of my marriage, I also wondered whether it was time to leave my job. At times, staying felt more than I could bear, and yet I stayed. Finally I felt I heard the distinct voice of God releasing me from my position. There was a quiet peace, and I just knew it was time to go. I didn't know what was next; I just knew change was coming and it would come from Him. And now I'm leading in a new church, where I've found it's okay not to be okay.

The song "Beautiful Things" did not turn out to be prophetic in the ways I had hoped. And I'm not here to tell you that everything turned out okay and "Look, I'm okay!" There are definitely days that is not true. But I can tell you that God brought me into a spacious place. And He is making, and will make, all things new.

The Greatest Grief: When We Lose Someone

Transitions like Brianna's and Lisa's bring grief of all kinds. You may not be experiencing this level of struggle, but I think we all know the sharp pain of loss, whether it's the bittersweet moment that you wave good-bye to your child on their first day of kindergarten, or the day you close your office door for the last time at a job you loved but know it's time to leave. Grief comes in all of these forms—moments of inevitable and good change but also in the unexpected sorrows that visit every one of us.

The ultimate suffering comes in the irreversible story of death. Grief is a sign that all is not as it will one day be. When Jesus comes to bring ultimate redemption to the world, the new heaven and earth will contain no mourning, crying, or pain. Grief is an unknown emotion to heaven.

But until that eternal reality, we live in the valley of the shadow of death. We live with the scary reality of our bodies slowing down and with the tenacious faith that our souls will continue on. My work in ministry has given me a poignant sideline seat to the particular shock and grief of families in the first days of losing a loved one. During that time, we come alongside family members to help them cope with the initial shock, make the arrangements, plan the service, and prepare for the final good-bye—for those days, it's as if the ministry team become part of the family, absorbing the shock waves of grief as they are felt, bringing a silent presence that says, *You are not alone.*

I've been with families as they've buried grandmothers

and grandfathers, mothers and fathers, sisters and brothers, husbands and wives. I've watched parents huddle over a casket small enough to cradle in their arms. I've seen mothers stroke the hair of their teenage sons one more time before saying good-bye. It feels like enough pain to drown in—deep, heavy pain sodden with tears, the deepest place of the valley of the shadow of death. In those moments, death itself looms like a dank presence in the room, clinging to every surface, covering its victims in despair. I've seen the ones left behind—the ones who have to go back into the sunshine that afternoon, who emerge, blinking, in disbelief that the world has not stopped in the shattering of the death of their husband, wife, mother, daughter, son, baby.

Yet in the midst of the kind of pain that takes your breath away, something else emerges. Out of that deep shadow—a place that seems lifeless and empty—something can grow. For some, what grows in that darkness is bitterness, anger, and despair. But for others, the darkness bores into their souls and creates depth. What feels like an abyss of loss and formlessness actually becomes a place where new life is planted. That new life doesn't come in the form of forgetting a loved one or even necessarily being grateful for the loss. But it does come in the sense of "numbering the days aright" . . . in somehow plunging headlong into the darkness and believing something important will emerge on the other side. My own sense of eternity has been deeply impacted by these people of depth. Somehow, their earthly losses illuminate the eternal aspects of their souls—their faith, their strength, their wisdom.

Tommy is one of those people. I first met Tommy through church. We were separated by age and stage of life, but I admired from afar the way he ran his business, loved his kids, and sought God. We had opportunities to work together on several projects at church, and he brought a settled confidence and deep humility that I found inspiring. But when Tommy's family entered a season of grief—the hardest kind—I was deeply moved by his example.

Tommy's Story

At age twenty, our daughter Perrin was in the spring semester of her sophomore year in college. Out of nowhere, she began having severe back pain. Her doctor thought it was a herniated disc, but then the pain got so bad that she went in for an MRI. When the doctors told us they thought it was lymphoma, we were in shock. They gave her a CT scan, which they said was routine. Afterward I remember the doctor coming into her hospital room. His face was white, and he couldn't quite figure out what to say. I knew something must be really wrong. I found him in the hall. He finally told me Perrin had kidney cancer, which was much, much more serious than what they expected. He gave me the basic stats of survival—incredibly bleak.

Within two weeks, Perrin had her kidney removed. It contained a tumor twice the size of the kidney itself. This started a seven-year battle of which there was virtually never a letup. I can think of one period of about six months when she felt good and we felt hopeful— but that was it. This wasn't just a battle with the cancer but with her almost constant pain. She nearly always felt sick.

The way Perrin found life in the midst of the cancer was almost like a fairy tale—if you wrote it as a story, people wouldn't believe it. Some of the turnarounds she had were completely beyond anything reasonable, from a medical standpoint. She met her husband two or so years after her cancer diagnosis. Joe fell in love with her with no reservations, knowing her prognosis.

We were always hopeful that God would heal Perrin. In fact, He showed up so often during her illness that we could recognize when He was at work. We knew we hadn't been abandoned. Whatever happened, He was in it. But many times I wrote in my journal to God, "I don't think I can bear another day. I can't go another day." Our hearts were so shattered. It was such a long, relentless battle. I don't have regrets. But there were times it was so hard to be around her. It just destroyed me to see her in such pain.

Every event in the final week of her life seemed to be orchestrated by God to prepare Perrin and us for the end. His hand was so evident throughout. I know many people come to peace with their loved one's end as it approaches, but that really wasn't the case for us. We really believed God was going to work some kind of miracle. In 2016—six years in—Perrin started a downward spiral from an already down place. In September she went into the hospital for a week. Through her illness, she had always looked so healthy that most people thought she was in remission. But that fall she looked gaunt. The week before Thanksgiving she just couldn't function, but even two days before she died the oncologist was bracing us by saying it might be a matter of months.

The end was surprisingly sudden. We were all with her when she died. It wasn't peaceful for me. It was horrible . . . horrible in *every sense. She was born on Christmas. She died at 6 p.m. the day after Thanksgiving, a month before her twenty-seventh birthday.*

When people talk about suffering or grief, the natural thing to do is to grade it according to severity. So people will tell us, "Yours is among the hardest." But suffering is suffering. Grief is grief. When you are in pain, you are in pain. I can acknowledge the unique difficulty of our situation, but it doesn't comfort me to think ours was particularly hard. Somehow in the midst of fighting it for nearly seven years with such poor odds, we were still surprised by Perrin's death.

Even though I was very hopeful and had a lot of faith, her illness and death have been a devastating, life-turned-upside-down loss that was relentless in every way. What's made a huge difference for both my wife and me is that we've given ourselves tons of space and tons of grace. Immediately after it happened, I was able to change my work schedule dramatically. I spent lots of time in quiet and a lot of time in the Psalms. Any place I could make life easier, I made it easier. Because life was constantly hard, we kept trying to find any respites that we could. I wrote in my journal—massive amounts. It was just a way to process everything we were thinking and feeling.

My wife and I stayed very much together through the grief even though we experienced things differently. I think that's where the grace came in. After Perrin died, we knew we were going to deal with it differently. We knew we couldn't judge the way we dealt with it—we just decided to be okay with it when we were not at our best. We'd be okay with tears. Okay with sadness, impatience, whatever. This is something we survive. It's nothing to be proud of, like "Boy, didn't we handle this great?" No. We just survived. And that's okay.

Do I wish I had superman faith to bounce back? To be honest, I don't even want that. It wouldn't feel real.

I can remember specifically journaling about what hope means in all of this. As Christians, we are supposed to hope in God, but does that mean I was hoping for Perrin to be healed? Hoping for an answer? I was never comfortable with what that meant. If it doesn't mean that, what does it mean to hope in God? What it came to mean for me was hoping in the character of God. It meant I would hope and believe and trust that whatever happened, God is good. Whatever happened, God is a redeemer. Whatever happened, God is kind and merciful. Whatever happened, God cares. Whatever happened, God is love. That meant I could let go a little bit at the end, and say, whether Perrin lives or dies, God is still good. God will be good, and God will bring good.

Hope means trusting in the character of God as a kind, gentle, loving, powerful Father who sees. That allows hope to be something that doesn't depend on the circumstances. Looking back, I can see so many instances of God's incredible goodness, gentleness, kindness, provision, and answered prayer—all in the midst of the fact that Perrin still died.

I don't know how to say this without sounding trite, but what's important to me has changed dramatically. I realize I thought of myself as a deep person before, but I wasn't. I just couldn't be. I hadn't been exposed to the depths. I like the fact that there's more to me—I'm pleased with that, although I'm in a new season of trying to understand that, to plumb those depths. I'm much less certain of who God is. I became aware that I believed that because of my faithfulness, there would be a limit to my suffering. I never in my wildest dreams imagined that God would allow suffering as difficult as this in my life. I thought my faithfulness to him earned a pass from this.

So when all this happened, it created a world of uncertainty. Our great pain wouldn't prevent something else from happening! All of a sudden anything was possible. And that was a really scary thing. So many times when we thought it couldn't get worse, it got worse. It felt Job-like. I've felt—with some self-pity and ego—like Job.

Too often we Christians tell a very dangerous story: If you come to Christ, you'll have ups and downs but everything will work together for good. That means all things have happy endings and life works out. That leaves a lot of people really lonely because this isn't their story—their life story isn't working out. I think sometimes the version of hope we preach is "hope that everything will work out." But the real Christian story is this: We aren't in control. This life is really hard. And our only hope is in the goodness of God and the reality of eternity.

When you look at it, we were never meant to hope in this life. Yet we still talk about it all as if this life works out. So what do you do when the end comes, if you believe the whole story is "life works out"? This life is a pinprick in eternity. So we really hope in the goodness of God and the reality of eternity. We can experience tastes of that eternity here and now, which God gives us to enjoy.

I've always been hopeful, but I haven't always felt hopeful. I feel more sadness. It's hard to experience joy. But weeping will last for a night, and joy comes in the morning. I do believe that joy comes in the morning. I do believe that. I believe God's goodness was evident in Perrin's story, which is crazy to say, because it was a horrible story by all outward measures. But oh my, how joy showed through. She experienced more joy in her cancer than most people experience in their lifetime. It was who she was, and it was the grace of God.

Living in the Gray

Stories from Scripture do not place a high priority on happy endings and perfectly executed resolutions. The last recorded words of the woman at the well are "Come, see a man who told me everything I ever did. Could this be the Messiah?" (John 4:29). We know *some* resolution from her story. We know that her statement changed the people in her town. We know that her words created interest, that the townspeople urged Jesus to stay with them, and that He stayed for two additional days. We don't know what He said—who He touched with His grace and truth, who He healed with His wholehearted power. But we do know that by the time Jesus and His disciples moved on, many in the town believed that Jesus was the Savior of the world. We don't know what happened to the woman who was living with a man who was not her husband. Did they settle down, get married? Did they buy a house with a white picket fence and have 2.5 kids? Did they go on to live a prosperous but faithful life? Did they get their happy ending?

We don't know. We won't know while we live on this earth. But maybe we do have resolution in this story and in all the stories of Scripture. Maybe resolution looks like this story—grace and truth and knowledge of God, a woman's life turned upside down, and the many people around her changed by her new story.

Perhaps we are focused on the wrong parts of the story's ending. Resolution may look like unfinished business and unreconciled relationships. It may look like continued gray scale in so many aspects of life—in our sin, in our struggle, in our suffering. Resolution may look like more uncertainty in this temporary life and more certainty about God. Resolution may look like bumps and bruises that remind us to fix our eyes not on what is seen, but on what is unseen.[4] Resolution may look like daily reminders of our own weakness, when we must choose to believe that *God is greatest, and He knows best* because we don't have any other options. Resolution may look like the unwritten parts of the story where our only true hope is *the goodness of God and the reality of eternity.*

Perhaps that's the only happy ending we truly need.

Keeping It Real

1. Have you ever experienced grief or guilt because of a transition in your life? Explain. What "old story" statements are you tempted to believe when you are in a transition?

2. What part of transitions are hardest for you? What does that teach you about your own weakness?

3. Tommy speaks of a dangerous story Christians often tell: that all things have happy endings. How have you handled the unfinished business in your own story?

4. What do transitions and endings teach you about what really matters in life?

The Beauty in Our Stories

We stood together under the hot July sun, the deck surrounding the pool jammed with people. If you'd observed this gathering from afar, you'd have had a hard time guessing the occasion. Some of the women wore dresses and hats; other people were in bathing suits and shorts. Kids bounced on their toes in flip-flops. Groups of adults gathered together under umbrellas, some by the cookies and pretzels on a card table. Moms found patches of shade where they could jiggle their babies gently, keeping them quiet as our pastor began to speak.

David, standing in waist-deep water, smiled at the strange gathering around the pool. He recited Galatians 2:20 from memory, the words flowing with casual confidence: "I have been crucified with Christ and I no longer live, but Christ lives in me. The life I now live in the body, I live by faith in the Son of God, who loved me and gave himself for me." One thing I appreciate about David is that when he reads Scripture, he sounds normal. He doesn't use that minister voice that I've always hated, the one that sounds as if someone is trying to make a holy voice, booming or singsongy or overly formal. When David speaks of the new life that's ours in Christ, he recites Scripture like he really believes it.

He gestured around the deck while addressing the people sitting on the edge of the pool, their legs dangling into the water. "The book of Hebrews says that 'since we are surrounded by such a great cloud of witnesses, . . . let us run with perseverance the race marked out for us.' Take a look around. The people surrounding you are family and friends who are here to celebrate your new life in Christ. These are the people who are most important to you in this new life that starts today."

Sitting on the edge of that pool were kids and adults—some teenagers, a married couple. All of them had an old story: the four-way broken story. And all of them believed that there was another story—a new story—being written on this sunny day in a suburban backyard, as they sat in their bathing suits and T-shirts, a sacred moment in a profoundly ordinary day.

Steve waded out to the middle of the pool first. Steve—a middle-aged guy who has a penchant for sarcasm but the heart of a servant. Steve—who's been through a lot in life. Steve—who has sat in worship services for years but who realized this year that he was ready to take this step. With hands firmly grasped between our pastor's own, Steve answered three questions:

Do you receive Jesus Christ as your Lord and Savior?
Do you confess yourself a sinner and rely on Jesus alone for God's forgiveness?

Relying on God's grace, do you commit to live as a
follower of Jesus, giving Him glory in accordance
with the Scriptures?

Steve said yes, nodding along as he entered the new story
with three "I do's." And with that, he was baptized in the
name of the Father, Son, and Holy Spirit, his body laid
down in a symbolic death, raised again in life—resurrected,
cleansed, and set free to the new story.

After Steve was Gina. She came to a women's conference
last year at the invitation of a friend. She went to church for
the first time that weekend. On this day she was baptized
along with her husband.

Then there was AJ. AJ has been in church his whole
life—and on staff at our church for years. But it was only in
the last several months that he'd experienced the strange and
wonderful presence of grace. Every time I'm with AJ, we discuss
grace. We talk about how grace is the ultimate rewrite,
how Jesus travels back in our stories to heal and transform
every aspect of our souls. AJ can't not talk about it. It's the
best thing that's ever happened to him.

There were dozens of adults being baptized that afternoon.
I knew some of their stories—and those were the ones
that made me cry with joy because I'm coming to understand
the transformative love that allows us to live into our
new stories. All of the baptisms also made me smile, and
wonder, about their four-way brokenness and about the four-way
restoration of Christ that was theirs. I thought about
the next months and years when God would patiently and

persistently move them toward Himself, in joy and in sorrow, in the undoing of the old and the creating of the new.

Then there were the kids—faces flush with youth and innocence, some shy in the intimacy of the moment as each nodded quickly in response to the questions. Three siblings were baptized together. And then the littlest one came, jumping into the pool with wild abandon like he could hardly wait to start his new story, swimming underwater and popping up next to the pastors, full of joy. Full of freedom.

My friend Pete was there, too, on the other side of David, holding those hands as they went under, his arm wrapping around them as they rose up to new life. I have twenty years of my new story, and Pete's been there the whole time. I'd realized as I drove up to this house that this was the very backyard where I came on Tuesday afternoons, the first summer I was a student intern. This backyard was where I led a Bible study with the bony-kneed group of middle schoolers to whom I'd first told my own broken, "it's not about the perm" story. Life is full of moments like this, holy intersections, shimmers of eternity.

In Greek, the language of the New Testament, there are two words for time. *Chronos* time is the source of our word *chronology*—it's the kind of time that's marked in seconds and minutes and days. Chronos time is the story that begins with birth and ends with death. But there's a second word for time in the Greek. It's *kairos* time, which is defined as "opportune time"—critical moments that matter in the deeper story of our lives.

In 2 Corinthians 5, the apostle Paul speaks of these kairos

moments in life. Jesus rewrites the story of which moments matter in life when framed by His work in the world. Because of Christ, we can be new creations. Because of Christ, we can have our stories reconciled to God. Because of Christ, we become messengers of freedom to a world so caught up in the enslaving lies of self-centeredness and sin (verses 17-20). And Paul caps it off by declaring,

> God says,
>
>> "At just the right time, I heard you.
>> On the day of salvation, I helped you."
>
> Indeed, the "right time" is now. Today is the day of salvation.
>
> 2 CORINTHIANS 6:2, NLT

Kairos moments are all around us. Kairos moments are the flashes of opportunity when we see the truth about ourselves, about our need for God, and about His presence in our lives. As insignificant as it might now seem in chronos time, opening my heart to those middle-school girls was a kairos moment. It's in such unexpected, often hidden, personal choices that we enter into the fabric of kairos, the place where God resides. These are the moments that define who we've been and who we are becoming. These are the moments that force us to choose between living into our new stories or retreating into the old. These are the moments that lead us to become wise or foolish, to become bitter or surrendered, to become fearful or trusting.

Kairos moments are the Polaroid pictures of our lives. They are snapshot moments that speak to something much deeper and more dynamic than one picture could ever capture. We have kairos opportunities every day, which fit into an album of snapshots that make up the story of our lives. And each of us has an opportunity to choose whether to engage in the moments that matter.

You are invited into the new story of your life. You are invited to discover those kairos moments, moments in which God chooses to invite you to the great something more of life in Christ. We find these moments in the little ways love moves among us. Sometimes these moments find us, right in the middle of the struggling or the suffering or the grief. This is the greatest work of our lives—to notice kairos, to own our great and redeemed stories, to press forward each day with intentional choices. "I set before you today life and prosperity, death and destruction" (Deuteronomy 30:15). When we choose Christ, we choose life. When we choose His life, we choose freedom. And with that freedom comes the new story, a story of depth, of purpose, and of redemption.

Each of us has an opportunity to choose whether to engage in the moments that matter.

In every moment, between every line, may your new story point to Jesus, who holds every hardship and orchestrates every joy.

Notes

CHAPTER 1: THE PROMISE

1. Natalie Wolchover, "Are Flat-Earthers Being Serious?" *Live Science*, May 30, 2017, https://www.livescience.com/24310-flat-earth-belief.html.
2. Dallas Willard, *Renovation of the Heart* (Colorado Springs, CO: NavPress, 2002), 240.
3. Don Richard Riso and Russ Hudson, *The Wisdom of the Enneagram* (New York: Bantam, 1999), 38.

CHAPTER 2: THE REALITY

1. Peter Kreeft, *You Can Understand the Bible: A Practical and Illuminating Guide to Each Book in the Bible* (San Francisco: Ignatius Press, 2005), xvi.
2. Ann Voskamp, *The Broken Way* (Grand Rapids, MI: Zondervan, 2016), 128.

CHAPTER 3: THE TRUTH

1. Dan P. McAdams, "The Psychological Self as Actor, Agent, and Author," *Perspectives on Psychological Science* 8, no. 3 (May 1, 2013): 272–95, https://www.ncbi.nlm.nih.gov/pubmed/26172971.
2. Ibid., 284.
3. *Oxford Living Dictionary*, s.v. "attitude," https://en.oxforddictionaries.com /definition/attitude.

CHAPTER 4: THE VOICES

1. Maria Paul, "How Traumatic Memories Hide in the Brain, and How to Retrieve Them," *Northwestern Now*, August 18, 2015, https://news .northwestern.edu/stories/2015/08/traumatic-memories-hide-retrieve-them.
2. If you don't know what a screamo band is, be glad. The word means exactly

what it sounds like: hard metal + screaming + emotions + usually a teenage front man with stringy hair and something to prove.

3. John Eldredge, *Waking the Dead* (Nashville: Thomas Nelson, 2003), 87.

4. Leonard Sweet and Frank Viola, *Jesus: A Theography* (Nashville: Thomas Nelson, 2012), 50.

5. *Merriam-Webster's Collegiate Dictionary*, 11th ed., s.v. "transfigure."

CHAPTER 5: THE VISION

1. William McGurn, "Dad Meets the Sexual Revolution," *Wall Street Journal*, June 12, 2017, https://www.wsj.com/articles/dad-meets-the-sexual -revolution-1497307294.

2. See Elisa Neuvonen et al., "Late-Life Cynical Distrust, Risk of Incident Dementia, and Morality in a Population-Based Cohort," *Neurology* 82, no. 24 (June 17, 2014): 2205–12, http://n.neurology.org/content/82/24 /2205; and Susan A. Everson-Rose et al., "Chronic Stress, Depressive Symptoms, Anger, Hostility, and Risk of Stroke and Transient Ischemic Attack in the Multi-Ethnic Study of Atherosclerosis," *Stroke* 45, no. 8 (August 2014): 2318–23, http://stroke.ahajournals.org/content/45/8 /2318.short.

3. Madeleine L'Engle, *Walking on Water: Reflections on Faith and Art* (New York: Convergent Books, 2016), 37.

4. 2 Samuel 22:25, msg

PART TWO: LIVING INTO THE NEW AND TRUE STORY

1. *The LPM Blog*, "SSMT 2017: Verse 13!" video blog post by Beth Moore, July 1, 2017, https://blog.lproof.org/2017/07/ssmt-2017-verse-13.html.

CHAPTER 7: THE LISTENING

1. National Public Radio, "Anne Lamott Distills Prayer into 'Help, Thanks, Wow,'" November 19, 2012, https://www.npr.org/2012/11/19/164814269 /anne-lamott-distills-prayer-into-help-thanks-wow.

2. Dallas Willard, *Hearing God: Developing a Conversational Relationship with God* (Downers Grove, IL: InterVarsity Press, 2012), 27.

3. Matthew 23:37; Luke 13:34 .

4. Willard, *Hearing God*, 42, italics in the original.

5. Brother Lawrence, *The Practice of the Presence of God* (Peabody, MA: Hendrickson Publishers, 2004), 31.

6. Kieran Kavanaugh and Otilio Rodriguez, trans., "The Sayings of Light and Love: Saying 158," in *The Collected Works of St. John of the Cross* (Washington DC: Institute of Carmelite Studies, 1991).

CHAPTER 8: THE BEGINNINGS

1. Rachel Gillett, "30 Scientific Ways Your Childhood Affects Your Success as an Adult," *Business Insider*, November 26, 2016, http://www.business insider.com/how-your-childhood-affects-your-success-as-an-adult -2016-11/#-29.

2. If you relate to this story and are interested in discovering how your temperament impacts your parenting style, I recommend the book *Different Children, Different Needs* (Colorado Springs, CO: Multnomah, 2004) by Charles Boyd with Robert Rohm.

3. Hundreds of personality tests have been developed, but three good online choices are http://16personalities.com, http://www.exploreyourtype.com /details, and https://www.123test.com/disc-personality-test/.

4. Exodus 34:7. See also Exodus 20:5; Numbers 14:18; and Deuteronomy 5:9.

5. *Oxford Dictionary of Difficult Words*, s.v. "redeem."

6. *Merriam-Webster's Collegiate Dictionary*, 11th ed., s.v. "redeem" (bold added for emphasis).

7. See Exodus 20:12; Proverbs 23:22; Matthew 15:3-6; and 1 Timothy 5:4.

8. Charles H. Spurgeon, "Scarlet Sinners Pardoned and Purified," sermon, April 1, 1894, Christian Classics Ethereal Library, http://www.ccel.org /ccel/spurgeon/sermons40.xiii.html.

CHAPTER 9: THE NEW LANGUAGE

1. Krista Tippett, *Becoming Wise: An Inquiry into the Mystery and Art of Living* (New York: Penguin, 2016), 15.

2. Bruce K. Waltke, *The Book of Proverbs, Chapters 1–15*, The New International Commentary on the Old Testament (Grand Rapids, MI: Eerdmans, 2004), 102.

3. Oliver Sacks, *Seeing Voices* (Berkeley, CA: University of California Press, 1989), 73.

4. Laura Starecheski, "Why Saying Is Believing—The Science of Self-Talk," *NPR*, October 7, 2014, http://www.npr.org/sections/health-shots/2014 /10/07/353292408/why-saying-is-believing-the-science-of-self-talk.

5. Thomas Merton, *No Man Is an Island* (Wilmington, MA: Mariner Books, 2002), 204.

6. *Hebrew-Greek Key Word Study Bible*, NIV edition, s.v. "anypokritos."

7. See chapter 13 in *She's Got Issues* and chapter 5 in *Brave Enough*.

8. *Cambridge Dictionary*, s.v. "sarcasm," http://dictionary.cambridge.org/us /dictionary/english/sarcasm.

9. Tippett, *Becoming Wise*, 29.

10. Brené Brown, "Rising Strong," August 6, 2015, Willow Creek Global Leadership Summit.

11. "Barth in Retirement," *Time*, May 31, 1963, http://content.time.com/time
    /subscriber/article/0,33009,896838,00.html.
12. Tippett, *Becoming Wise*, 24.
13. Ibid., 25 (italics in the original).
14. Colossians 1:16; John 8:12

CHAPTER 10: THE CHAPTERS

1. Emily V. Gordon and Kumail Nanjiani, "A Girl, a Guy, and a Coma,"
   Glamour, August 2017, 105–108.
2. Timothy Keller, *Walking with God through Pain and Suffering* (New York:
   Penguin, 2013), 2, 13, emphasis added.
3. See the study note for John 4:18 in the *NIV Study Bible*.
4. See 2 Corinthians 4:18.

About the Author

Nicole Unice is an author and Bible teacher who has a passion for bringing God's Word to life in a personal and relevant way. Her training as a counselor informs her work, as she emphasizes the importance of facing our own reality and embracing the transforming power of God's grace.

Invitations to speak have taken Nicole around the world, and her books come to life through her popular video curriculum series found on RightNow Media. Her heart belongs to Hope Church in Richmond, Virginia, where she serves as ministry director and leads Praxis, a full-time ministry residency program for young leaders.

Nicole holds degrees from the College of William and Mary and from Gordon-Conwell Theological Seminary. She loves creating space for spiritual growth in the everyday rhythms of life with three children, two pups, one husband, and a whole community of twentysomethings who regularly raid her fridge.

If life seems harder than it should,
get ready to find new strength and confidence! Join popular Bible teacher and counselor Nicole Unice to discover why the struggle is real . . . and what to do about it.

The Struggle Is Real Participant's Guide: This is a six-session workbook designed for use with *The Struggle Is Real DVD Experience*, based on the book by Nicole Unice. A great resource for church groups, Bible studies, and anyone who's ever felt life just shouldn't be this hard!

The Struggle Is Real: Nicole Unice provides practical tools to help you navigate daily ups and downs and offers ways to rewrite your struggle into a new, God-centered life story. Discover how to take the hard, hurtful, and confusing moments and turn them into opportunities to grow in wisdom, strength, and joy.

The Struggle Is Real DVD Experience: Designed for use with *The Struggle Is Real Participant's Guide*, this six-session DVD curriculum, based on Nicole Unice's book, teaches how to practice gratitude, make godly choices, and live each day with confidence and contentment. Also available through online streaming at www.rightnowmedia.org.

To learn more from Nicole and access additional resources, visit her online at www.nicoleunice.com.

rightnow MEDIA

THE EVERYDAY STUFF THAT DRIVES YOU CRAZY ... IS ABOUT TO TRANSFORM YOUR LIFE.

Some days living up to the whole good-Christian thing seems impossible. You do the right things (well, most of the time), but you just don't feel changed by your faith. Deep down, you're still dealing with the everyday issues—control, insecurity, comparison, fear, and anger (along with its cousin, unforgiveness)—that hold you back from living free and loving well.

The good news? You don't have to "fix" yourself. You have access to the power of Christ. His power can transform your everyday weaknesses into your greatest strengths and gifts. In *She's Got Issues*, you'll join Christian counselor, ministry leader, and regular mom Nicole Unice on a new journey of learning to better understand yourself and others by exploring how these issues affect us ... and why we don't have to settle for letting them win.

CP0574

Bring *Brave Enough* to your
community, and start living

BOLD and FREE

Brave Enough

Find the courage to be who
you are . . . not who you wish
you were. Discover what it
means to live a brave-enough
life, fully alive and confident
in who God made you to be.

978-1-4964-0136-6

Brave Enough DVD Group Experience

Join Nicole on an eight-week
journey to being brave enough
right where you are.

978-1-4964-0138-0